# The Medway

## Sketches Along The River

based on Samuel Ireland's

*Picturesque Views on the River Medway (1793)*

David Addey and Shally Hunt

Foreword by The Viscount De L'Isle MBE

Prospero Books
46 West Street
Chichester
West Sussex
PO19 1RP
UK

A CIP catalogue record for this book is available from the British Library.

Printed and bound in Great Britain.

ISBN 1 902320 06 9

# Contents

List of colour illustrations     5

List of black and white illustrations     6

Foreword     9

Acknowledgements     10

Artist's comments     11

Author's comments     13

Preface     15

Introduction     19

Map of the Medway     24

Garrison Point, Sheerness     25

The Hoo Peninsula     30

Minster Abbey     41

Queenborough     46

Cooling Castle     51

Gillingham     53

Brompton     56

Upnor Castle     58

Chatham     62

Rochester from Frindsbury Hill     69

Frindsbury     77

Temple Farm, Strood     81

Lord Darnley's Mausoleum at Cobham Park     90

The Remains of Halling House     99

Malling Abbey     102

Leybourne Castle     106

Hop Gathering     108

The Friars and Aylesford     111

Kit's Coty House     115

Allington Castle 117

Maidstone 121

Boxley Abbey 129

Leeds Castle 132

East Farleigh 136

Barming Bridge 137

Teston Bridge 138

Wateringbury 141

Mereworth Castle 142

Nettlestead Place 144

Twyford Bridge 148

Branbridges 150

Tonbridge 152

Penshurst Place 163

Hever Castle 167

Groombridge Place 171

High Rocks and Tunbridge Wells 175

Bayham Abbey 185

Bibliography 190

# List of colour illustrations

Plate  I          Garrison Point, Sheerness

Plate  II         Minster Abbey

Plate  III        Cooling Castle

Plate  IV         Upnor Castle

Plate  V          Chatham

Plate  VI         Rochester from Frindsbury Hill

Plate  VII        Temple Farm, Strood

Plate  VIII       Lord Darnley's Mausoleum at Cobham Park

Plate  IX         Leybourne Castle

Plate  X          Malling Abbey

Plate  XI         Aylesford

Plate  XII        Maidstone

Plate  XIII       Boxley Abbey

Plate  XIV        Leeds Castle

Plate  XV         East Farleigh

Plate  XVI        Teston

Plate  XVII       Nettlestead Church

Plate  XVIII      Twyford Bridge

Plate  XIX        Tonbridge

Plate  XX         Hever Castle

Plate  XXI        High Rocks

Plate  XXII       Penshurst Place

Plate  XXIII      Bayham Abbey

# List of black and white illustrations

| | |
|---|---|
| The P.S. Medway Queen | 12 |
| In Hoo Boatyard | 14 |
| Cranes at Thamesport | 18 |
| Grain power-station from Queenborough | 29 |
| The Hogarth Inn, Grain | 31 |
| Maunsell Forts, Shivering Sands | 34 |
| A Thames barge | 35 |
| Kingsnorth power-station | 36 |
| A Palmerston fort | 38 |
| The Church of St James, Grain | 40 |
| Shurland Hall, Minster | 45 |
| The Guildhall, Queenborough | 47 |
| The old 'Radio Caroline' off Queenborough | 50 |
| A glimpse of Brompton | 57 |
| Gazebo in Upnor | 61 |
| Old paddle-tug at Chatham | 65 |
| The P.S. Kingswear Castle | 66 |
| A Thames barge | 68 |
| A conglomeration in Limehouse Reach | 70 |
| The M2 motorway bridge from Cuxton | 70 |
| A corner of Rochester | 76 |
| All Saints' Church, Frindsbury | 77 |
| Temple Farm, Strood | 82 |
| Oyster boats off Strood pier | 84 |
| Old lock gates, Strood | 86 |
| Signal box at Snodland station | 88 |
| Ferry Cottage, Snodland | 89 |
| Cobham Hall | 92 |
| The Church of St John the Baptist, Halling | 100 |
| Rugby Cement works at Halling | 101 |

The Cascade, Malling Abbey 105

A glimpse of the Friars, Aylesford 114

Kit's Coty House, near Aylesford 116

Dutch barge at Allington Lock 118

Courtyard in Allington Castle 120

The Archbishop's Palace, Maidstone 123

Leeds Castle from the east 135

East Farleigh station 136

Mereworth Castle 143

Nettlestead Place 144

A distant view of Yalding 149

Tonbridge School from near the Medway 155

In the churchyard, Penshurst 166

Groombridge Place 174

Adam's Well near Langton Green 177

The Chalybeate Spring, The Pantiles, Tunbridge Wells 184

The old gatehouse, Bayham Abbey 188

# Foreword by The Viscount De L'Isle MBE

The village of Penshurst has its origins in Jutish times, when communities gathered around churches sighted at nodal points, such as the confluence of the rivers Medway and Eden at Penshurst. In 1339, Sir Stephen de Penchester sold his Estate to Sir John de Pultney, who then built his defended manor house on the rising land to the north of the Medway beside the church, where both buildings stand side by side. Gone is the Jutish forest, but we are still blessed with enough woodland to conceal most of the developments built down the ages. There are a multitude of enchanting views of Penshurst and the river from standpoints around the valley.

The Upper Medway Flood Relief Scheme, completed in 1983, protects Tonbridge and the land below it. Modern technology has enabled the Environment Agency to predict the volume of water flowing down the river. A barrier at Leigh allows the river water to be impounded when necessary. The water backs up the valley through Penshurst, forming an enormous lake up to an area of 900 acres, briefly transforming the landscape to one akin to the *wasser* Schloss of Germany. Improved flow of the river means fewer floods, but every few years one is able to glimpse a spectacular view of the house and village rising above the vast area of flood water before it disappears in a few hours.

I am lucky enough to possess a collection of engravings, prints and pictures of Penshurst Place and its surroundings over the ages; these images reveal how the house has changed. When Samuel Ireland painted Penshurst in 1793, it was in such a parlous state of repair that one visitor reported, 'the mansion is now deserted and will probably, before another generation passes, be only known as a ruin'. At the end of the 18th century, this comment could have applied to many of the historic buildings in Ireland's book, *Picturesque Views on the River Medway*. Two hundred years later, Penshurst still stands, cared for by five succeeding generations. Most of the subjects depicted by Samuel Ireland are in much better condition today, although few are still privately owned. Close inspection of the Penshurst sketch will reveal the changes in structure between Ireland's view and that of David Addey. This book will not only delight our generation but be of great value to our grandchildren.

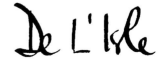

# Acknowledgements

Inevitably, the journey of discovery that David and I have just completed has called for co-operation from many people throughout our travels. Without exception, a telephone call or a tentative knock on a door, has been greeted with interest and enthusiasm. A question to an Information Bureau or a total stranger has been courteously answered - and, unlike Samuel Ireland, on no occasion have we been refused entry.

In an effort to reduce errors and omissions to a minimum, I have sought the assistance of owners of many of the properties described and, in particular, I would like to thank Sister Mary David of Malling Abbey, Alan Albert of Leybourne Grange, Roy Tucker of Nettlestead Place, Stephen Best-Shaw of Boxley Abbey, The Rev. Robin Murch of Queenborough, Sylvia Hammond of Cobham Hall, John Hesketh of Barham Court, Christopher and Abigail Peny of Bayham Abbey, Andrew de Candole of Groombridge Place and Lord De L'Isle of Penshurst Place, who has also been kind enough to write the Foreword.

Ian Beavis of Tunbridge Wells reference library has given me invaluable assistance and so, too, have the librarians at Rochester, Tonbridge and Maidstone. The many friends who have lent me books, given anecdotes and general encouragement deserve especial mention, together with Carpenter Editorial Services who have spent hours on the unenviable task of proofreading my drafts. Some of David's paintings are in private ownership and we are grateful to their owners for allowing them to be reproduced. Last, but not least, thanks to my husband, both for his encouragement over this project, and the time and trouble he has taken to guide me along the Medway from the windswept marshes of the Hoo Peninsula to the fertile landscape of Bayham Abbey.

# Artist's comments

The topographical artists of the 18th and early 19th centuries must have thoroughly enjoyed their explorations, and there are times when, with the frenetic pace of today's life and changing scenery, I wonder why I have become involved in projects of this nature. True, in earlier days, there would have been disadvantages with matters such as travelling and accommodation, but it is the subjects and the environment which they portrayed that make me envious. Just imagine a countryside without motorways, housing estates, railways, pylons, street lights - and the Medway with sailing barges and bawleys instead of the ubiquitous, characterless motorboats. It is surprising though, that even after 200 years since Ireland's journey along the river, there are still a few corners that have remained largely unchanged. You will discover these as you read this book.

We have been able to visit all the properties depicted or mentioned by Ireland. Some of these are in private ownership and rarely open to the public, but their owners have been more than generous in allowing us access and giving freely of their time and knowledge. Without such unstinted co-operation we would not have been able to complete our task.

In one or two cases, today's viewpoint has had to be different from Ireland's who, on several occasions, took considerable artistic licence. It is possible that he did not visit all the properties and may have relied on descriptions by other travellers.

Man and Nature have conspired to change the scenery since Ireland's days, Man has built and destroyed; in fact, he has to destroy in order to build. Except for the occasional severe storms and floods, Nature takes time to change and in the views depicted on our journey, the growth of trees has been its most noticeable contribution to the landscape.

It is, perhaps, unfashionable to be a topographical artist today when events and scenes can be recorded more rapidly with the camera. The 'contemporary' artist is not taught to observe and to draw in a sketch book with a pencil - that is too plebeian - and it is far more newsworthy to produce something that will disturb or shock.

But there is still a place in the History of Art for the quiet observer who seeks nothing more than to enjoy his work and to pass on some of that enjoyment to others.

Next time you speed past the Medway in your car, halt awhile and take a walk along its banks; you will be very surprised at what you discover. And take a sketchbook with you.

*The P.S. Medway Queen*

# Author's comments

When David asked me to write the text for a book on the River Medway, my heart sank. From school days I recalled dreary pictures of the Medway towns, which established early prejudices. The high level of pollution, from agriculture and industry, has since earned the river the nickname, the 'Mudway.' Therefore, it was with low expectations that I set out on this journey of discovery, following in the footsteps of Samuel Ireland, from the Isle of Sheppey to Bayham Abbey. Speeding along the motorways and trunk roads that have robbed the river of its usefulness as a highway, most of us have no idea how much beauty and interest we are missing. To discover the riches of this river, it is necessary to search deep into the industrial heartlands of the Medway towns, to walk along the river banks and marshes, and to be on the river itself, preferably in a sailing boat, canoe or paddle-steamer. As the book reveals, the traveller will be well-rewarded.

Change over time is inevitable, but today's developments are so rapid that it is difficult to keep up with them. The container port at Sheerness, the new housing estate on St Mary's Island, and the Medway Tunnel, are just a few examples. The river, used in Ireland's time predominately for mercantile trade, is now mainly a playground. New estates, marinas, heritage dockyards and leisure complexes, have covered fields where once cherries, corn, and hops grew in abundance, while the romantic sails of fishing-boats and barges have been replaced with pleasure-boats and container ships.

Two hundred years after Ireland selected his *Picturesque Views on the River Medway* there is a feeling of nostalgia. As the millennium approaches, we look back through rose-tinted glasses to the 'security' of the past, and put our heritage on a pedestal. The River Medway reflects Kent's long and eventful history more than any other single feature in the county. The *venerable* buildings, described by Ireland in 1793, were privately-owned, many in a state of decay and disrepair. They were not open to the public and, on several occasions, Mr Ireland was disappointed because access was forbidden. Today, it is a very different story. The only way many of these great castles and houses can survive, is by opening to the public and providing as many income-generating activities as possible. This has enabled the buildings to be restored and improved, giving enjoyment to the general public, and ensuring that they survive for posterity.

Without its industry the Medway might well become a theme-park. Instead, it is a rich mix of agriculture, industry, history, living and leisure. The Environment Agency ensures that the water quality is rigorously monitored, setting limits on all permitted discharges. The river's shrinking natural environment is carefully conserved, for today we realise the importance of preventing our 'Garden of England' becoming a toxic compost heap. Recreation and industry go hand-in-hand, as we learn to use this *gentle river* in a new way.

Unlike Samuel Ireland, we have explored the Medway in depth, and found it a rewarding experience. I hope this book will encourage many others to follow in our footsteps and discover for themselves the delights of these *Picturesque Views*.

*In Hoo boatyard*

# Preface

Little is known about Samuel Ireland's beginnings, and the date and place of his birth are not recorded. He is thought to have been a self-educated weaver from Spitalfields, London. His intellectual and artistic abilities served him well and, like Hogarth, he dealt in prints and drawings, teaching himself to draw, etch and engrave. His artistic work, unlike Hogarth's, is described as 'amateurish' by the *Dictionary of National Biography,* but he did have one picture, *A View of Oxford,* exhibited at the Royal Academy in 1784. He specialised in landscapes, backed by bright, plain skies, or buildings in minute architectural detail set in pleasant surroundings. These picturesque scenes pleased the taste of the age and won him some popularity.

Like so many 18th century gentlemen, he developed a taste for collecting books, pictures and curiosities, a hobby which became an all-absorbing passion. His methods were not all beyond reproach for, in 1787, he was accused of bribery by Horace Walpole of Strawberry Hill, who wrote:

'Mr Ireland, a collector, I believe with interested views, bribed my engraver to sell him a print of the frontispiece, has etched it himself, and I have heard, has represented the piece, and I suppose will sell some copies as part of the forty.'

In 1794, Ireland also increased the status of a part of his collection by issuing *Graphic Illustrations of Hogarth, from Pictures, Drawings, and Scarce Prints in the Author's Possession.* Some of the plates were etched by himself. A second volume appeared in 1799, and it is thought that Ireland, wilfully or ignorantly, assigned to Hogarth some drawings by other artists.

In 1790, Ireland published *A Picturesque Tour through France, Holland, Brabant.* The two handsome volumes were dedicated to Francis Grose, author, artist, and antiquarian, and sold well. In 1792, encouraged by this success, Ireland followed with *Picturesque Views on the River Thames* and, in 1793, by *Picturesque Views on the River Medway* dedicated to the Countess Dowager of Aylesford. In 1795, using the same successful format, Ireland produced *Picturesque Views on the River Avon,* and, in 1797, a further volume on the River Wye.

In 1791, Ireland was sufficiently well established to move to 8, Norfolk Street, The Strand, London. In this pleasant house by the River Thames, friends like Thomas

Lindey, part owner of the Drury Lane Theatre, brought him into contact with a stimulating circle of actors and dramatists.

In a book called *The Fourth Forger* by John Mair, the middle-aged Samuel Ireland is described as a 'plump, pert little Polonius of a man'. His increased prosperity enabled him to entertain the rich dilettantes of the day, who would admire and possibly purchase some of his growing collection of rare prints and books. His household consisted of a housekeeper called Mrs Freeman, his son, William Henry and unmarried daughter, Jane.

In 1794, Samuel Ireland's modest social success was greatly enhanced by the mysterious discovery of important papers relating to William Shakespeare. Unknown to him, these flawed forgeries, known as the *Shakespeare Manuscripts*, were the work of his only son, William. Such was the 18th century thirst for discovery, and the Shakespeare mania of the time, that they were pronounced genuine, even by those professionals who should have known better.

More of these Shakespeare 'discoveries' continued to pour from young William's pen for several years. They included personal papers and letters by the Bard, a manuscript of *King Lear*, another of *Henry II*, and an unknown tragedy entitled *Vortigern*. William was only nineteen when he produced his first audacious forgeries and, initially, merely meant to impress his father, who had always dismissed him as an intellectual lightweight.

However, the pretentious and gullible Samuel Ireland, Esq. set about masterminding the rapturous hysteria that followed these 'discoveries'. William pretended that the papers came from a mysterious and highly invisible gentleman, and Samuel, delighted at this good fortune, became an unwitting Mephistopheles, innocently encouraging his son to produce more and more forgeries. Naturally, an increasingly complex tissue of lies and deceptions followed.

Samuel's moment of glory was short-lived, and the publication of *Miscellaneous Papers Hand and Seal of William Shakespeare* sealed his fate. The Age of Reason had reflected on the forgeries, and came to its senses. An Irish barrister and well-respected literary critic, called Edmonde Malone, published a vituperative book on the 'spurious' *Shakespearean Papers,* in which he levelled every possible textual, lexicographic and historical criticism against the Papers. After this blistering attack, the believers were gradually outnumbered by the sceptics. Prior to this, Ireland had persuaded Sheridan to put on the 'newly discovered' Shakespeare tragedy, *Vortigern,* (written by young William) at Drury Lane. It says much for the author that, although inferior to most of Shakespeare's plays, many believed it to be genuine. The theatre was packed for the first night but, fanned by a hostile press and the publication of Malone's book, its first performance was the last.

This marked the beginning of the end for father and son. William confessed to his father that he was the sole forger, but Samuel, in his contempt for his son's abilities, and pathetically fierce conviction that fate could not so utterly betray him, refused to believe the truth. William then published his confessions in *An Authentic Account of the Shakespearean Manuscripts,* frankly admitting his authorship of the forgeries. If William had hoped for literary recognition, he was disappointed; the confession was considered merely a product of his vanity, or of his father's cowardice. Later that month, Samuel Ireland published his *Vindication of his Conduct respecting the Publication of the supposed Shakespeare MSS.* It suffered the same fate as his son's, and was disbelieved.

The Ireland manuscripts remained scurrilous fodder for journalists, and Samuel's reputation was now in tatters. Harried by the press and suspected by his customers, his health began to fail. He continued his lonely campaign for belief in the Papers to the end. In 1797 he published *An Investigation into Mr. Malone's Claim to the Character of a Scholar or Critic,* in which he vented his futile anger against his victorious antagonist. This did little to ameliorate his situation, and in a final attempt to regain some credibility, he published William's two plays, *Vortigern* and *Henry II,* with introductions in which he avowed his innocence of forgery.

Meanwhile, William estranged himself from his father, and rather than commit suicide like his hero, Chatteron, sank into impoverished oblivion, ending his days merely as a literary hack. However, he left twelve poems, several novels and a handful of biographical and miscellaneous compilations which have endured. Of the latter group, one book called *England's Topographer on the County of Kent,* published in 1830, describes Allington, Chatham, Upnor, Rochester, Sheerness, Tonbridge and Tunbridge Wells. The artists are such well-known men as Burford, George Shepherd, and T.M. Baynes. In imitating his father's topographical writings and, having more proficient artists doing the sketches, William appears to be enjoying some revenge.

The literary public never forgave this clever young man for exploiting their deepest sensibilities. William died in Suffolk Place, London, in 1835 at the age of sixty-four, maintaining his father's innocence and his own sole authorship to the very end. His forgeries follow those of Lauder, Macpherson and Chatterton.

Samuel Ireland, Esq. of Norfolk Street, London, died in 1800, physically unequal to his unrelenting struggle to make the world believe that he was totally ignorant of the deceit, and believed in the authenticity of the manuscripts as much as even the most credulous. Ironically, he is remembered today not so much for his artistic, acquisitive and writing abilities, but for his part in the audacious charade of his son's Shakespeare forgeries, which, for a time, duped even the cognoscenti. Samuel's books, paintings, drawings, prints and various curiosities were sold by auction in May 1801.

*Cranes at Thamesport*

# Introduction

The wanton tide in wreathing volume flows,
Still forming reedy islands as it goes;
And, in meanders, to the neighbouring plain,
The liquid serpent draws its silver train. (Sir Richard Blackmore)

Over the centuries it can be said that the world has come to the Medway, and the Medway to the world. The river has been a nursery for seamen; Francis Drake learnt his seamanship in the tidal estuary of the Medway, and Nelson not only boarded his first vessel here, but his flagship, H.M.S. *Victory* was built at Chatham in 1765.

Historically, Kent has been a landing-stage for invaders. Julius Caesar and his forces were the first Roman invaders in 55 BC, but the true conquest of Britain was undertaken by Emperor Claudius, who fought the native tribes of Kent at the Battle of the Medway in 43 AD. This significant, but little-known battle, has recently been commemorated by a monolithic chunk of ragstone sited on the east bank of the Medway opposite Snodland Church. The Romans then settled and stayed for three centuries before departing, leaving a civilising imprint of roads, villas and artefacts along the lower reaches of the river. *The Saxon Chronicle* states that Kent was founded by three Germanic peoples known as the Jutes, the Saxons and the Angles. In 450 A.D. the Jutish warriors, led by Hengist and Horsa, were invited by the hard-pressed ruler, Vortigern, to fight as mercenaries against the savage Picts. Having beaten the Picts, they decided to stay, forcing the Britons to leave Kent. Hengist died in 488, and his son, Aesc, succeeded to the Kingdom. By the end of the 5th century, the first of the English Kingdoms was established. The rampant horse, emblem of Kent, is said to have originated with the brothers Hengist and Horsa. It is thought that these were nicknames, Hengist meaning a stallion, and Horsa, a wild horse. As this animal was a popular figure in Scandinavian art, it is likely that the brothers would have decorated their longship with a rampant horse.

In 597, Pope Gregory sent his missionary, St Augustine, to bring Christianity to the Anglo-Saxons. Kent became the cradle of Christianity in the south of England, and this new religion made erratic but persistent progress. Its growth was responsible for some of the *venerable* buildings Ireland sketches and writes about in his book, *Picturesque Views on the River Medway*. Many of these ecclesiastical buildings are in ruins today, but the great cathedrals of Canterbury and Rochester attempt to keep Christianity alive in an increasingly secular society.

In the 9th century, marauding Vikings raided and plundered Kent and elsewhere, and in 1066 William the Conqueror defeated Harold at the Battle of Hastings. These centuries of conquest and re-conquest produced a rich culture with firm links to European civilisation. The "Kentish Men" were supposedly descended from the Saxon invaders, while the "Men of Kent" from the Jutes. These strong and independent settlers seem to have adopted the Medway as a political frontier between the different tribes, and even today the distinction endures with the "Men of Kent", who settled to the east of the river, and the "Kentish Men" to the west.

In 1066, when William the Conqueror marched into Kent, the "Men of Kent" met him at Swanscombe carrying branches to conceal their numbers. William was amazed, thinking some miraculous wood was moving towards him. These sylvan warriors then demanded either peace and their ancient liberties, or war 'most deadly' if these were denied them. William was so impressed by their courage that he allowed them to retain their ancient privileges. The county motto became INVICTA, meaning 'unconquered' and, unchanged today, it is written under the logo of the rampant white horse.

However, the pride of these "Men of Kent" suffered a brief, but humiliating, incident during the invasion of the Medway by the Dutch in 1667. The Napoleonic Wars, at the end of the 18th century, posed another invasion threat, and the Martello towers and forts built round the coast of Kent bear witness to this. In 1940 the Battle of Britain, fought in the air over Kent, helped prevent a German conquest under Hitler. The Channel Tunnel was a more cordial invasion, built to narrow the gap between England and her European trading partners. It was inaugurated on 6 May 1994, by Queen Elizabeth II of England and President Mitterand of France.

The 18th century historian, Hasted, wrote these words in his *History of Kent*, published in 1797:

Among the different counties of England, few have been more enriched both by art and nature than the county of Kent. Its situation was so well adapted for commerce and trade, and by the bravery of its inhabitants it was preserved as an entire kingdom for about four hundred years . . . its inhabitants were far more civilised than those of other parts of Britain . . . from the establishment of the Church, learning and religion were spread throughout the county by the most eminent and distinguished men of the kingdom, to the great increase of good government and of society in general.

William Camden, in his *Britannia*, published in 1739, describes the county of Kent as,

abounding with meadows, pastures and cornfields, that it was wonderfully fruitful in apples, as also cherries . . . The county had many cities and towns, tolerably safe harbours, and some iron mines; but the air was somewhat thick from the vapours rising from the waters.

Samuel Ireland used both these sources extensively in his text.

The origin of the name Medway has many explanations. Ireland chooses the following:

*The Medway, originally denominated Vaga by the ancient Britons, from the Saxons received the additional syllable of MED, signifying Mid, or Middle, to denote its course through the centre of the kingdom of Kent; and hence its compound appellation Med-vaga, or Medwage, which is now modernized into Medway.*

The Romans settled near the Medway, and for the next four centuries a regular water-borne trade developed. A period of unrest followed their departure, and regular commerce along the river did not resume until the Norman Conquest. Kentish ragstone, a mix of sand and lime, was used in the building of the many Norman castles erected at this time, including the Tower of London. Later, iron and timber from the High Weald was transported down river to Chatham and London for shipbuilding, cannon and munitions. Textiles and, later, paper were manufactured along the Medway, and then taken to London by barge. Since Roman times, agricultural produce such as corn and hops, cherries and oysters, were shipped along the Medway and the Thames to feed the growing London markets. In the 17th century, imported goods included coal from Newcastle, dairy produce from East Anglia, and bricks from Holland.

Kent today is still known as the 'Garden of England'. However, in the 19th and 20th centuries, houses and factories rather than crops have crept over the fertile banks of the Medway. Meadows and pastures have become bricks and mortar; first the railway, then the roads, have superseded the river as a means of transport. Now, pleasure-boats are almost the only traffic on the Medway. The air, rather than the water, is thick with vapours round the industrial towns of Snodland, Cuxton, Strood, Chatham, and Gillingham. Since Ireland's day, the paper, oil and cement industries have flourished, while fishing and farming have declined. In today's disposable society, waste is a major industry. Kent County Council has applied for planning permission to build two waste-to-energy incinerator sites at Allington and Kingsnorth, to recycle Kent's four million tons of waste per annum and help prevent the 'Garden of England' becoming a toxic compost heap.

At the end of the 20th century, the lower reaches of the Medway are synonymous with industry. The towns of Strood, Rochester, Chatham and Gillingham merge into one great industrial conglomeration, and their polluting chemicals, together with the increased quantity of domestic effluent, have adversely affected the once *sweet waters* of the river. However, recent efforts to improve the water quality have been effective, for the Medway is now a waterway for living and leisure. Gone are the sturgeon and the salmon, but boating, fishing and walking have all been carefully nurtured, and many stretches of the river are surprisingly unspoiled.

Upstream from Rochester, the ancient villages of Wouldham and Burham sit alone on marshy waste land, gazing across to the belching chimneys of Snodland and Cuxton. Wouldham Church takes its place in history as the last resting-place of Walter Burke who, with Captain Hardy, was supporting Nelson when he died on H.M.S. *Victory* at the Battle of Trafalgar. This waste land is now a Site of Special Scientific Interest. Aylesford, where the first 'Battle of Britain' was fought in the 5th century, draws its old houses protectively round the medieval bridge, only a stone's-throw from the largest recycling paper mill in Europe, the busy M20, the Channel Tunnel rail link, and the grey outskirts of Maidstone.

From Maidstone to Tonbridge, Samuel Ireland would have felt relatively at ease. The medieval ragstone bridges at Teston and East Farleigh still grace the river, which now flows through hop-gardens and orchards much as it did in the 18th century. In 1823, William Cobbett wrote of this stretch: 'From Maidstone to this place (Meryworth) is about 7 miles, and these are the finest 7 miles that I have ever seen in England or anywhere else.'

Once through the traffic and bustle of a much-changed Tonbridge, the Medway still passes through some of the most unspoiled and attractive countryside in Kent.

# The River Medway

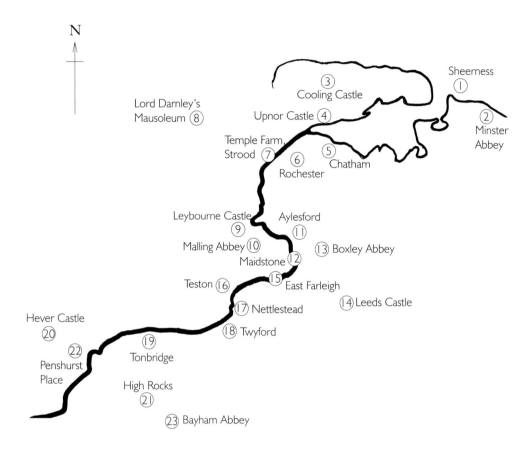

Sheerness ①
Cooling Castle ③
Upnor Castle ④
Lord Darnley's Mausoleum ⑧
Minster Abbey ②
Temple Farm, Strood ⑦
⑤
⑥
Chatham
Rochester
Leybourne Castle ⑨
Aylesford ⑪
Malling Abbey ⑩
⑬ Boxley Abbey
Maidstone ⑫
⑮
Teston ⑯
East Farleigh
⑭ Leeds Castle
⑰ Nettlestead
Hever Castle ⑳
⑱ Twyford
⑲
Penshurst Place ㉒
Tonbridge
High Rocks ㉑
㉓ Bayham Abbey

Note: The italics in this text are quotations from Samuel Ireland's book *Picturesque Views on the River Medway*.

# Garrison Point, Sheerness

*The entrance to our river . . . is well defended by the extensive battery and fort at Sheerness . . . The site on which this fort was built, in the reign of Charles I, was only a swamp . . . but this entrance being an avenue both to the river Thames and our great naval arsenal at Chatham, it was thought of such importance . . . as to be afterwards drained and made capable of receiving a small fort of twelve guns.*

Garrison Point, on the north-west tip of the Isle of Sheppey and opposite the Isle of Grain, is the perfect site for a fort to guard the mouth of the Medway with its safe anchorage on the Nore sandbanks. The marshy, windswept Isle of Sheppey is bordered by the Swale (which divides it from the mainland), the Thames Estuary and the River Medway.

A reincarnated Samuel Ireland would have trouble in recognising the subject of his first sketch at Garrison Point. Interestingly, Ireland's sketch is identical to one in Hasted's History of Kent, entitled *The East View of Sheerness.* Today, the stout battery wall, crouching roof-tops, and saluting chimneys of the old fort, have vanished. So, too, have His Majesty's ships-of-the-line, their skeletal masts ranged 'in ordinary' at the mouth of the Medway, waiting to defend 'King and Country'. The expression 'in ordinary' meant ships lying on the river without rigging or sails. These would be stored at the dockyard ready for refitting, should the ship need to go into action with the fleet.

The old fort was demolished in 1860, and a new fort erected, which was operational until 1956. This semicircular construction now sits rusting on Garrison Point, and is owned by the Medway Port Authority with a radar station on its roof. Although the stiff breeze no longer fills the sails of fishing smacks going about their business, the coast of Essex is still visible, demarcating the north flank of the Thames. The skyline on every side is filled with the silhouettes of 19th and 20th century industry, much of it obsolete. On the horizon, the oil storage tanks of Shellhaven Point and Canvey Island gleam like molars in a watery mouth, swallowing the giant container ships that fill the estuary with steel.

Sheerness means 'bright headland', yet on a grey day at the close of the 20th century, it appears a collage of metal and concrete, chimneys and cranes, decaying history, litter and wind. At night, neon and arc-lights fuse past and present as they illuminate the ghostly ruins of Napoleonic defences, drunken pillboxes and steel sheds.

The tattered remnants of the dock side area of Sheerness, known as Blue Town, still stand in the shadow of the high dockyard wall built in 1827. The original houses and timber cabins, erected by the dockers themselves, were painted in blue naval regulation paint, which gave the town its name. The first dry dock in Sheerness was built in 1708 and, by 1754, there were sixteen blue houses. This number swelled to 130 by 1792, when obsolete men-of-war, or hulks as they were known, were brought to the foreshore, providing cheap accommodation for dockyard workers and their families. In 1820 a serious fire destroyed all the remaining cabins, but they were rebuilt by 1823.

Today, only a few of the old houses remain. In spite of an improvement scheme in the area in 1991, Blue Town is in a state of terminal decay. The pier master's house stands beside the disused dock railway, opposite a scaffolding depot, littered with dirty trucks, stacks of disused tyres, assorted timber and steel poles. Two moribund pubs, The Lord Nelson and The Jolly Sailor, make a last stand at each end of West Street. Alongside the crumbling magnificence of The Royal Fountain Hotel, a nightclub is for sale. Only the pubs and an Adult Playshop are open. A few cobbles are visible in the narrow ghost-filled twittens between the silent houses. One business which still thrives amongst the decay, advertises itself as 'Kent's largest concrete ornament manufacturers'. Behind a high brick wall, gnomes, wishing-wells, rampant lions and sailing-boats wait to decorate somebody's garden.

Naval Terrace, a row of faded Georgian houses next to the old chapel and the imposing dock gates, gives a taste of former prosperity. Now, bounded on one side by imported cars, and on the other by railway sidings, steel, and gas works, they unwillingly degenerate. The indigenous population here has its own creed and culture.

Outside Tesco's superstore at Sheerness, where Ireland would have made his sketch, the contemporary scene resembles the perimeter fence of a concentration camp. Mini-pylons, topped with powerful lights, stand like sentries behind a litter-filled fence, where the ground drops steeply into a channel of stagnating water.

Rounding the headland of Garrison Point on the Medway side of the island, a large area of mud-flats on the Lappel Bank has been reclaimed between Sheerness and Queenborough. At one time, waders, geese and sheep used to feed on the mud and marshland, but early in the 1990s a new sea-wall was built. Reject sections of the Channel Tunnel, cast on the Isle of Grain, have been used to form the landing-stage where the huge container ships can unload thousands of motorcars. A colourful kaleidoscope of foreign vehicles lines the tarmac of 'Rats Bay', oozing over the hinterland, awaiting collection. Across the road, the steel mill, with its noisy freight train, adds to the industrial scene.

The Sittingbourne to Sheerness railway came to Sheppey in 1860 and ran via Queenborough to Blue Town. It was electrified in 1959 and is still in use now. The pier, square-rigged in steel, was built for ferries to visit our Dutch neighbours, and from 1976 to 1994 the Olau Line took passengers to Vlissingen. Today there are only cargo ships. Head and shoulders above the landscape stands the megalithic power-station on the Isle of Grain, an exclamation mark on every horizon.

The defences at Sheerness today are not to keep out the Dutch but the powerful and constantly threatening sea, where a massive sea-wall curves its concrete arm for several miles along the shingle. The metal masts and eerie superstructure of the Second World War munitions Liberty ship, *Robert Montgomery*, is another very real and visible threat at low tide. Lying on the Nore, a sandbank and anchorage at the mouth of the Medway, the wreck, too explosive to defuse, literally bites the bullet.

Samuel Ireland lived in unsettled times. Towards the end of the 18th century, Great Britain stood alone against a revolutionary France and her Spanish and Dutch allies. These countries all possessed a fleet, potentially a serious threat to Britain's naval supremacy. In 1797, four years after Samuel Ireland's book was published, the Dutch were forming a large invasion fleet for the French army which could sail against Britain at any time. Only the Royal Navy stood between England and an army of 30,000 men.

At this time, there was deep discontent amongst Britain's seamen. More than half the lower deck of the swollen war fleets was comprised of men who had been either forcibly impressed or recruited from debtors' prisons. Conditions on board ship were appalling; discipline was harsh and brutal, food poor and inadequate, pay small and irregular and shore leave rarely granted. Sheerness was the scene of the notorious Nore Mutiny, when sailors of the Nore Command, led by Richard Parker, rebelled against the inhuman conditions in which they lived. None of the mutineers' demands were met, and the mutiny was quelled after only nine days. Richard Parker was hanged on his ship, *The Sandwich*, '. . . his body hung in chains on the most conspicuous land in sight of the ships at the Nore.' Parker requested that he release a white handkerchief when ready for the execution to take place. The crew would then fire a gun from the bow, signalling the gang of seamen on the deck below to haul up the rope which was tied in a noose round Parker's neck. In a final act of defiance, Parker did not release the handkerchief to give the signal that he was ready for the execution; instead he jumped to his death from the scaffold, catching everyone unawares. The mutiny was not, however, a total failure, for it brought home to the general public the very real injustices suffered by men of the Royal Navy, and conditions gradually improved.

Most of the houses in Sheerness were built for the dockyard workers in the 19th century. Behind the sea-wall leading to Minster, it is noticeable that many houses are below sea-level, with views from the upper windows only. Red-shank, dunlin and ringed plover search for food on the shingle tide-line; huddles of clinker-built boats are corralled near the amusement arcades. Echoing shrieks from the swimming-baths outdo the vociferous oyster catcher, fishing-rods sprout on the shingle, day-glo wind-surfers dart across the waves like fireflies, while youths on roller-blades fly along the sea-wall yelling, 'Watcha 'Enry 'ees 'ere! Gotcha Kev. Comin' dad!'

Behind the Pugin-decorated Roman Catholic church, an elegant terrace of Georgian houses nestles in a time warp where Ireland would have felt at home. A poster in one window invites the passer-by to 'Clairvoyance Cocktails' followed by a 'Psychic Supper'. Spiritualism is rife on Sheppey.

*Grain power-station from Queenborough*

# The Hoo Peninsula

The Isle of Grain is the bulbous nose on the windswept Hoo Peninsula, *in form resembling a ham, which, in the Saxon, is hoh or ho; and thence probably the origin of the name of this place,* our 18th century artist informs us. Yantlet Creek scars the nose, and once divided the Isle of Grain from the main peninsula when it was truly an island. This barren creek made a handy short-cut between the Thames and the Medway. It was still an island in Ireland's time for, he notes, *it has been thought expedient to dam up this water of Yentlet in order to avoid the increase in smuggling* and, where the power station now stands, *on the border of the creek . . . a considerable salt work has been erected.* Historically, this flat marshy piece of land has an inhospitable reputation. Ireland could not resist the following anecdote written by the 16th century historian, Holinshed:

'He that rideth in the hundred of Hoo,
Besides pilfering seamen, shall find dirt enow.'

The forbidding Hoo Peninsula was not just bleak marshland and salty water, for the 'ague', now known to be malaria, was a real killer. Although today the area is disease-free, the ferocious mosquito persists to perpetuate the story of rich brides and avaricious grooms. In past times, the new husband, marrying only for money, would take his wealthy bride to the Isle of Grain for the honeymoon. After a suitably romantic interlude, he would make excuses to leave her for a week or two, hoping that the mosquito would do its worst. If the virulent ague set in, he would return, having lost a bride and gained a fortune. This anecdote did not escape Samuel Ireland's pen. Of the Hoo Peninsula he writes:

*It is still notorious for its aguish air; which is said to have removed many a yeoman's wife, who was not a native of the spot, and to have enabled him again to seek another by the operation of the same causes, soon again to meet the same fate.*

Inhospitable though it is, Hoo has had its share of famous visitors. In 1732, Hogarth and four high-spirited friends went on a five-day pub crawl through Kent. It was agreed that Hogarth should produce some sketches, while another member of the group, Ebenezer Forrest, should write a light-hearted account of their journeying, known as *Hogarth's Peregrinations.* Forrest writes:

. . . we left Hoo, and an agreeable widow landlady who had buried four husbands. (This sounds like bride's revenge.) As we travelled along this charming country, the weather was exceedingly pleasant . . .

The artist and his friend were obviously hungry when they reached Grain, and, with only passing reference to the church, Forrest continues,

' . . . we stopped at the Chequer Ale House, kept by Goody Hubbard, who entertained us with salt pork, bread, butter and buns, and good malt liquor.'

*The Hogarth Inn, Grain*

Unlike the church, the pub has changed little, and is now called The Hogarth Inn in memory of the artist's visit.

In 1882 the Hundred of Hoo railway line was opened. Free trips from Cliffe to Gravesend were given to local children as part of the opening festivities. One paper reported that for many inhabitants of Cliffe it was the first time they had ever seen Gravesend, although the town was only five miles away. A branch line from Hoo Junction took the train to Cliffe and across the peninsula to Grain, where it terminated on a wooden pier known as Port Victoria. The Hundred of Hoo railway never flourished, but gained a certain status when, in 1890, the Royal Corinthian Yacht Club moved to this port. Queen Victoria herself also used the pier-head for embarking and disembarking from the royal yacht, *Victoria and Albert*. A special train was routed from Windsor for her use, and she could alight onto the pier itself with only a few steps to walk to the waiting yacht. She found, in this remote spot, that she could come and go unobtrusively. Just as well, as on one occasion when the pier was out of use, she was winched from shore to ship in a bath chair. Other prestigious visitors were the German Kaiser, King Edward VII and Queen Alexandra. All that remains of the pier today are a few timber piles, visible at low water.

Due to its position at the mouth of the estuary, Grain has played an important part in defence through the ages. Grain Tower was built in the second half of the 17th century to co-ordinate fire with the Sheerness Batteries, block the Medway, and oppose enemy landings on the Isle of Grain. The remains of the fort, built in 1867, can still be seen.

Since the Dutch invasion of 1667, the defence of the Medway has not been neglected. In 1914, the Fifth Battle Fleet, 20th century updates on Ireland's men-of-war, was once again in the Medway anchorage, ready to combat any German moves in the English Channel. Tragically, in the next few months, both the battleship, *Bulwark,* and the minelayer *Princess Irene,* exploded at their moorings with the loss of most of the officers and crew. For Ireland, the defence of the realm was of paramount importance, and in jingoistic tone, while surveying the men-of-war lying on the Medway below Gillingham Fort, he wrote:

Plate I

Garrison Point, Sheerness

Plate II

Minster Abbey

Plate III

Cooling Castle

Plate IV

Upnor Castle

*. . . a sight that must animate the breast of every Englishman, to retain that dominion which their fathers left them in possession of, and to convince them . . . of the absurdity of fortifying by land, when these wooden walls . . . can be so readily called forth on any sudden attack of the enemy.*

Ireland felt that the ruinous fort at Gillingham was superfluous to requirements, forgetting that warships with their cargo of munitions are very vulnerable.

This century, the peninsula has certainly played its part in both World Wars, with an experimental seaplane station on the Isle of Grain, and an airship factory at Kingsnorth. Shortly after the seaplane station was abandoned by the R.A.F, the same area was taken over by the Admiralty as their Armaments Depot. This meant that ships, entering Chatham dockyard for refits, could unload their ammunition and rearm when leaving.

In 1929 Grain was used as a gun-testing station, much to the disgust of the locals who suffered damage to property and nerves. The Isle of Grain became the 'Isle of Grin-and-bear-it.' In spite of their protests they had to bear it until the mid-fifties.

Further eerie mementoes of the strategic importance of the Medway estuary in wartime are the Redsand Towers, known as Maunsell Forts, just off Sheppey. Used for anti-aircraft fire during the Second World War, these rusting pillboxes on stilts perch like aliens on Shivering Sands. Now derelict, they achieved a certain notoriety in the pirate radio world of the 1970s.

*Maunsell Forts, Shivering Sands*

Industry also leaves its scars. The Kent Oil Refinery built in 1952 by BP on the south side of the Isle of Grain had berths for seven tankers in Saltpan Reach. This mammoth enterprise was short-lived, and the refinery was closed down in 1983, leaving a legacy of steel mushrooms dotted over the horizontal landscape.

The Hoo Peninsula remains flat and windswept, and sea mists still descend without warning, wrapping the marshes in a damp shroud, blotting out the power-station, oil and gas storage tanks, and jetties of the busy container port. Naturalists and bird watchers have replaced the smugglers of Yantlet Creek, and the farmers of Hoo still cultivate the land - and we hope they look after their womenfolk better.

The Medway's narrow entrance opens into a wide mouth, where the marshy saltings of Stoke Ooze float in the upper palette. Under the tongue of navigable Medway, larger islands, bordering Stangate Creek and the Swale, echo their history with gruesome names: Burntwick, Deadman's and Slaughterhouse Point.

*A Thames Barge*

In the last century there was a quarantine station on Burntwick Island and the headstone on the grave of Sidney Barnard, R.N. is still visible, although rapidly disappearing under the silt. His story is worth recounting as it illustrates the high mortality rate from tropical diseases in the 19th century. In 1845, Her Majesty's ship, *The Eclair*, was engaged in antislavery duties in West Africa, when some of her crew contracted yellow-fever. The ship's captain and three naval surgeons all died, and twenty-nine-year-old Sidney Barnard was taken on board at Madeira, having volunteered to serve as a temporary surgeon until the ship was safely back in England. The fever-ridden ship arrived at the quarantine station on Burntwick Island on 2 October 1845, and Sidney Barnard, worn out with sickness and fatigue, died one week later. By this time 74 out of the complement of 146 had died. A century-and-a-half later the lonely grave of this brave man is sinking fast into the marsh silt.

When gales and spring tides whip the grey-green sea into excited, frothing ridges, a bubbling cauldron overflows onto these 'sinking' islands. Lines of restless gulls mark the perimeters, and isolated trees and shacks cling to higher ground.

Today, the flat horizon is broken by the industrial architecture. Silhouetted steel gantries and giraffe-like cranes tower above the lighters and cargo ships. Yachts, motorboats and paddle-steamers are toys in a bath beside the power-stations of Kingsnorth and Grain. The massive linear blocks of Kingsnorth are crisscrossed with steel tubes sloping gently to the water's edge. The exhaling chimney of this colossal energiser, imitates clouds as it reaches for the sky.

*Kingsnorth power-station*

In Ireland's day, dreadful hulks were anchored off Sheppey; old men-of-war, stripped of their masts, rigging and guns. They were draped in a rough canvas, to keep out the worst of the weather, and were used as prison ships. *The hulks,* Ireland says, *are occupied by sixty or seventy families, and chimnies of brick are raised from the lower gun-deck, which give them the whimsical appearance of a floating town.*

His cosy description gives the reader no idea of the living hell on board some of these ships. Without the weight of masts, rigging and guns, the hulks rode much higher in the water, permitting scuttles to be cut into the sides of the hull to communicate with the orlop deck. This lowest deck, measuring about 38 metres in length, 12 metres in width and 1.5 metres high, would house about 460 men in double or even triple layers of hammocks. The air was fetid, and there was so little ventilation it was hard for a candle to burn. In these cramped and filthy conditions, there was no comfort, very little food and nothing to do. Disease was rife, and many prisoners, including boys, would practise self-harm in order to get into the sick bay, although conditions there were little better. The damp environment, exacerbated by river mists, meant the ships were truly rotting hulks. In spite of this miasma of degradation, a few prisoners were able to make the most beautiful artefacts from bone, rough wood and straw. Some have survived, and the sophistication and craftsmanship of these inlaid boxes, cribbage sets, dice and gaming-boards are a remarkable testament to the spirit of man in adversity.

The prisoners of war (mainly French) were expatriated after 1815, and the *whimsical floating towns* finally disappeared from the Medway. As the 20th century approaches its close, the burgeoning prison population has meant that there is once again a prison-ship afloat, not on the Medway, but in Portland Harbour on the Dorset coast.

Late 20th century hulks are the gargantuan container ships, which load and unload their cargo at Thamesport on the Hoo Peninsula and Sheerness. Their brightly-painted lofty decks are piled high with multicoloured boxes containing every luxury, and resemble a floating Manhattan.

A little way up river, in Long and Gillingham Reach, the enduring forts of Dartnet and Hoo float on round, green islands like turreted brick cakes. They were built by Palmerston in the 1850s to keep the French at bay. With hindsight, this paranoia is not unreasonable, and both Pepys and Ireland would have approved of this vigilance.

*A Palmerston fort*

In the late 17th century, the Dutch with their powerful navy were a threat to Britain. In 1651, economic rivalry at home and in the East Indies, brought Britain into conflict with Holland, and a series of naval clashes continued well into the 1660s. In 1665 there had been skirmishes between the English and Dutch Africa Companies. Charles II mobilised a powerful fleet to block the Zuyder Zee, and so contain the Dutch. This failed and, on 8 June, 1665, Pepys reported in his diary that the Dutch were off Harwich. A naval battle ensued at Lowestoft and, although the English fleet was victorious, worries about Dutch reprisals prevailed. Pepys confided to his good friend, Mr. Evelyn, 'we have not a ship at sea to do them (Dutch and French) any hurt . . . the Kingdom is like to be lost, as well as the reputation of it for ever'.

In 1666, the Dutch were again menacing the coast of Essex. On Monday, 10 June 1667, Admiral De Ruyter had *dispatched his vice-admiral, Van Ghent with seventeen sail of his lightest ships, and eight fire ships up the Medway,* where they successfully attacked Garrison Point, and *razed the beggarly fort,* wrote an indignant Samuel Ireland 117 years later. The Dutch pressed home their advantage, sailing on up the Medway to destroy several prestigious naval ships at Chatham. In a final coup de grace, they towed away the *Royal Charles,* a fine 82 gunner that had brought the king back from exile. Ireland's account of this debacle makes sorry reading:

*A strong easterly wind and spring tide having carried them with resistless force, the chain laid across the river was presently broken . . . this calamity was likewise attended with the destruction of the Royal London, the Great James, and the capture of the hull of the Royal Charles.*

The chain mentioned by Ireland was an important feature of the river's defences, and would probably have stretched across the water about 700 yards at a point below Gillingham Church, to somewhere midway between Folly Point and Hoo Ness in Gillingham Reach.

The victorious Dutch then returned unmolested to Sheerness, and coolly *sailed away in triumph for the coasts of Essex and Suffolk.*

On that black Monday, the inhabitants of Grain woke to find themselves invaded by a few of the high-spirited crew of one of the Dutch vessels from the large fleet dispatched up the Thames. Help for the beleaguered inhabitants came from Sheerness, in the form of twenty-six musketeers of the Royal Scots. Meanwhile, the Dutch seamen set about looting the church, battering down the great door and making off with the communion silver. If caught, the looters knew they would be hanged so, when warned of the approaching musketeers, the silver was returned to Grain Church. Today, the repaired door still stands, and the silver, dated 1594, remains in use. Other versions of the story maintain that the massive church door resisted the Dutch attempts to break it down, and the looting seamen retreated empty-handed.

Having suffered an invasion and losing some of her most prized men-of-war, English pride was as damaged as her ships. Chatham dockyard was promptly enlarged, and the Medway defences strengthened, to ensure that this humiliating episode in naval history could never be repeated. In Ireland's words, the Dutch were *a power that contested with us the empire and the sea and whose ports lay very near our coasts.*

*The Church of St James, Grain*

# Minster Abbey

*Elevated in its situation, rich in verdure, and fruitful in corn . . . no unpleasant retreat for the summer months.*

Along the sea-wall from Sheerness to Minster, the flatness is relieved by grass-covered cliffs rising gently from the shingle beach, although the late 20th century bungalows of Minster, sprawling down the hillside, threaten to envelop what *verdure* still exists. The crumbling cliffs no longer grow corn, doubtless due to the erosion, which was just as bad in Ireland's day. He describes an acre of land which fell onto the beach below *leaving the corn entire on its surface,* which was later reaped on the beach *with no small loss to the owner.*

A bald path leads up the green slopes into the town. The latticed windows of bungalows frown at one another across the street; gangly youths wheel and screech on mountain-bikes, their shouts drowned by barking dogs and revving engines. At the summit of the hill, the ancient minster sits demurely on a verdant island, hemmed in by pubs, car parks and petrol stations. Beyond the ancient stones of the 12th century gatehouse, a cream cylindrical toilet with wraparound door, perches uneasily among the fag-ends and tired grass. The Working Men's Club shares the tarmac with bottle-banks and litter-bins. Two small girls play ride-a-cock-horse on an iron cannon, made in 1700, at the forge then situated in the west gatehouse of Robertsbridge Abbey. The wind stirs dead leaves from the mature trees near the perimeter of the churchyard; stout iron railings firmly remove the abbey and its grounds from the 20th century. From the southwest corner, the gatehouse and church look much the same as in Ireland's sketch. Today, the great south doors are locked, the tombstones are propped round the edge of the churchyard, and a handsome church hall lies to the north of the abbey. Boys and girls loll beside their bikes, munching crisps. There is a long, stone wall which connects the old gatehouse to the abbey church. This annoyed Samuel Ireland because it concealed views of the Medway estuary, views *as would otherwise give a splendid idea of the naval and commercial character of our nation.* The patriotic Ireland proudly tells his readers that the Medway estuary, *by the depth of its channel and softness of its bed, is rendered not only the best, but the only perfectly secure harbour for large ships in the kingdom.* Using a little artistic licence, the offending wall is omitted in Ireland's sketch.

In his text, the church is described as *a small but venerable structure* and the 16th century monument to Sir Thomas Cheyne is admired by the artist, noting sadly that the metal inscription plate is missing, *said to have been removed for better security.* Vandalism, it seems, is nothing new. Our troubled artist adds earnestly:

*One would hope, for the credit of these public repositories of the dead, and for the honour of the church . . . that this rapine must have been committed at some earlier and more licentious period.*

Now, the abbey is locked and visitors are requested to collect the key from the vicarage, with strict instructions not to let anybody in with them.

The urban sprawl disappears as the ground drops sharply to the south. Only isolated prison-blocks interrupt the view across the flat marshlands of this 'island of sheep'. In the distance, the Swale is a silver ruler, dividing Sheppey from mainland Kent. Buildings obscure any views of the Medway, but the tall chimney of the Isle of Grain power-station towers skywards, an outward and visible sign of the material demands of the late 20th century. Pylons punctuate the flatscape, looping their high-tension cables to the rim of the horizon. The lowering sun glints on cars, metal warehouses, steel chimneys, arc-lights and the river.

Minster may not have a McDonald's, but can boast a memorable Sexburgha. The abbey church of Minster-in-Sheppey was founded by Queen Sexburgha in A.D. 664, making it one of the oldest places of Christian worship in England. Ireland tells us that *this monastery suffered considerably from the Danish invasions and was at length nearly destroyed by them in which state it remained till the year 1130.* It was then rebuilt by Archbishop Corbeuil in the 12th century and dedicated to St Mary and St Sexburgha. Its fortunes declined and, at the Dissolution in 1536, it was acquired by Sir Thomas Cheyne. The abbey's annual revenue was by then *no more than one hundred and twenty-nine pounds seven shillings and ten pence.*

Like every visitor to this abbey, Ireland's attention was held by the canopied altar-tomb of Baron Robert de Shurland, who died in 1327. The robust knight lies in full armour, an armed page at his feet and the skull of a horse rising from waves of stone at his side. The artist sketches this monument, and recounts, in detail, one of the *ridiculous tales . . . very current among the common people, however contemptible in itself,* propagated about this knight and the horse's head.

Contemporary visitors may enjoy the following ballad, composed in the 19th century when the abbey was heavily restored.

I'll tell you now of knight so bold
De Shurland was his name.
He fought against the infidel,
To Sheppey he brought fame.
One day when in tempestuous rage,
A priest of God he slew,
But through wild waves to pardon rode
This gallant knight I knew.

On his return to island shore,
Urging his weary steed,
He met an ancient withered crone,
Her hair like wild seaweed.
'Take heed, take heed!' the old witch cried
Her eyes afire with hate,
That noble horse will carry you
To Satan through Hell's gate!
But Robert straightway drew his sword
'Avaunt old crone' quothe he,
Then killed his horse with skillful thrust
And laughed lightheartedly.
'Look now, old witch' Sir Robert cried,
Sheathing his bloodstained blade,
'The evil ones can do their worst,
From your foul curse I'm saved.'

As time went by, the lusty knight
Forgot the fearsome spell,
Until one day on stony strand
He spied the horse's skull.
'You cannot harm me now,' he cried,
And kicked contempt to show.
But bone as sharp as dagger's point
Caused Robert's blood to flow.

The doctors tried with might and main
And all the arts they knew,
But Robert's soul burst earthly bonds,
And through Hell's gate it flew.
So now beneath my ancient stones
His body lies entombed.
But stories of his deed still live
In Sheppey's hearts enthroned.

A good pupil of the Age of Enlightenment, Ireland hastens to explain away any magic in the story.

*The horse's head may have been probably placed there to express his affection for a favourite horse which had been the means of saving his life, by swimming with him across the Swale.*

\* \* \* \* \*

*About four miles east of Minster, and within the manor of Shurland, stands the mansion many years since occupied by the Cheineys, but anciently by the Shurlands beforementioned.*

Shurland Hall, built by Sir Thomas Cheyne in the reign of Elizabeth I, is situated just outside the village of Eastchurch. Ireland tells us that Sir Thomas used materials brought from Chilham Castle, *formerly the residence of that family.* He dismisses the manor in one sentence: *Shurland House is spacious, and has an air of solemn grandeur; but in the late repair it underwent, having lost its embattlements, gothic windows and other ancient decorations, it is rendered no longer worthy of attention as a specimen of antiquity:* a view that is not held today, for the mansion is currently snugly wrapped in polythene sheeting undergoing major restoration. The accompanying sketch is from a recent photograph.

*Shurland Hall, Minster*

Robert Shurland, that 'lusty knight', would no doubt have been proud to know that it was on his estates that man fulfilled his centuries-old ambition to fly. The little village of Eastchurch was the cradle of aviation. The first officially recognised flight in Britain, by a powered aircraft, was made on 2 May, 1909 by Lord Brabazon from Sheerness. Short Brothers built a factory at Leysdown-on-Sea, just a few miles south of Shurland Hall, and Lord Brabazon won the Daily Mail prize of £1,000 for the first Briton to fly an all British aeroplane for one mile over Britain in October 1909. This was a remarkable achievement in a machine which looked like a dragonfly on wheels.

Samuel Ireland would surely have applauded the brave men who launched themselves into the air in these spindly contrivances. Now, the aerodrome at Shellness near Leysdown is in use as Stanford Hill prison, and only a monument in Eastchurch informs the visitor of Sheppey's major part in aviation history.

# Queenborough

*The town, notwithstanding the celebrity of its architect has, from the transitory condition of all sublunary things, no traces of its original form.*

Ireland's indifference to the town may have had something to do with a lack of victuals, for he found hospitality sadly lacking during his visit in 1793.

*. . . but in this once famed place, so royally recommended that comfortable refreshment should be wanting, may well afford matter of surprize to the traveller. So near the sea, we neither found oysters though in season, nor even mutton, from the abundance of which this island is said to have received its denomination of Shepey.*

This was surprising, as in Ireland's day there were oyster-beds in the Swale. Today's traveller would have no such problems. The smell of fish pervades South Street, and the seafood shop does a good trade. In earlier days, the overpowering smell would have been one of fertiliser, as rotting bones from all over Kent were carted up the High Street to the fertiliser factory, where maggots and all were ground into bone-meal. As this factory came into existence in 1623, it is cause for speculation as to how many convicts, smugglers, fevered seamen, prisoners and mutineers played a passive role in making Kent the 'Garden of England'.

In the 17th century, Queenborough was the main port and trading town of Sheppey until the fort and naval dockyard were built by Samuel Pepys and Charles II at Garrison Point, Sheerness. Queenborough is definitely a town with a past. Associated with it are many of famous names: Edward III, John of Gaunt, Francis Drake, Henry VIII, Elizabeth I, Cromwell, and Nelson. Since then the town's fortunes have declined.

There are a number of late 17th and early 18th century houses remaining in the High Street. In 1793, the year Ireland wrote his book on the Medway, the elegant Guildhall in Queenborough was built. Lady Hamilton, living at Church House for a time, was conveniently placed for Nelson to visit her while he was staying at 149 High Street. In 1805, Nelson's body, preserved in a barrel of brandy, was brought into the estuary in his flagship, *Victory,* after the Battle of Trafalgar. The body was transferred to the Sheerness Commissioner's yacht, and taken up the Thames to Gravesend to its final resting-place in Westminster Abbey.

*The Guildhall, Queenborough*

If Shurland Hall is presently hiding under wraps, Queenborough Castle has certainly vanished. Donald Maxwell, in his book *Unknown Kent,* dismisses it as 'a water-tank on a light bump in a railway station': a fairly accurate description for, without the information board, today's visitor would need a vivid imagination.

However, the status of Queenborough Castle lasted well into the 16th century. In 1582 it became the official residence of the Lord Warden of the Cinque Ports when Sir Thomas Cheyne held that prestigious office. He entertained Henry VIII, and the castle was sumptuously refurbished for the occasion.

Samuel Ireland concentrates on the castle's heyday, with Hasted's *History of Kent* at his side, in the absence of a late 20th century information board:

*This town and castle are reported to have been built from a model or design of William of Wyckham, surveyor of the works to Edward III . . . to quote the king's own words, 'as being pleasant in situation, the terror of his enemies, and the comfort of his subjects.' The borough, with the right of representation in parliament, was added by him in honour of Philippa of Hainault, his queen, thence called Queenborough.*

The castle was built of stone around 1361, a novel design for its date, although not suitable to withstand cannon fire. It was the last of the 'Bow and Arrow' castles with maze-like approaches, giving excellent killing-grounds.

By the reign of Charles I, the castle had fallen into a state of dilapidation. After Charles's execution, it was surveyed for Oliver Cromwell who deemed it 'useless for cannon'. Parliament, therefore, disposed of the castle to a Mr. John Wilkinson, an expert demolition speculator, who expertly demolished it stone by stone. Even Ireland had to admit that

*no traces are remaining . . . The moat that surrounded it is still visible. In its center is a well forty fathom deep, which remained a long time choaked up; but in 1723 it was opened by order of the commissioners of the navy, and has proved of great utility to this place, as well as to the inhabitants of Sheerness.*

Ireland makes a sketch of the castle *from a scarce print by Hollar, said to be the only genuine view extant, that has been engraved.* This 'genuine view' is now reproduced on an excellent information board by the 'small green bump' where the castle once stood. The castle, unlike Shurland Hall, was certainly a *good specimen of antiquity* with six battlemented towers, inner and outer courts, twelve ground floor rooms with forty or fifty above. The still visible, capped-off castle well supplied the town with water and, earlier this century, it was used to supply the steam trains.

In the 1990s, the present incumbent of Queenborough Church, the Reverend Robin Murch, was told the following story by an elderly resident of the town. In the 1860s there was no piped water, so it was a precious commodity. At this time, a local fisherman, called Bill Ost, lost his sight and, to earn his keep, used to draw water from the well with two buckets suspended on a yoke round his neck, and deliver it from door-to-door. Being familiar with the town and its families, he would recognise voices and 'feel' the pathways with his feet. He charged the purchaser one penny per bucket. In those days there was no dole, and Bill ended his life in the rough and simple poverty typical of Queenborough at that period.

In the reign of Elizabeth I, Queenborough was still on the royal map; Good Queen Bess was inclined to pay surprise calls on her loyal subjects. She would descend, without a word of warning, together with her large, glittering retinue, and expect to be entertained in the spectacular manner to which she was accustomed. When, on a warm afternoon in 1582, Her Majesty crossed the Swale and rode into Queenborough, the town was naturally unprepared. As the royal procession entered the High Street, the worshipful mayor was off duty doing a spot of DIY on his thatched roof in his gardening clothes. Having a bird's eye view of the royal procession clattering up the High Street, he must have hoped he would soon wake up. Realising he was not dreaming, he mopped his sweating brow with a dirty hand, wobbled down the ladder, and bade Her Majesty a worshipful welcome. The sight of his large behind, clad in threadbare breeches, made such an impact on the queen that her parting gift was £50.00, 'to buy the mayor a new pair of breeches, or equivalent.' This set the local tongues wagging. After a few Chinese whispers, the residents of Queenborough decided that 'or equivalent' must mean an elephant, for no breeches could ever cost such a sum. The story of the Queenborough elephant lives on, and rumour has it that the memorial park was built to house this non-existent royal gift.

Today, the glory that was Queenborough survives, if only in name. The 19th century pub, across the road from the castle, is called The Queen Philippa. It backs onto the creek, very conveniently situated for Edward III and his Dutch queen to sail over to Holland and visit the in-laws.

Now the creek is a jumble of assorted boats in various stages of disrepair. Rusty fishing vessels, peeling houseboats and fibreglass motor-cruisers lounge on the mud at low tide, showing their age. The old houses in the High Street back onto the gently curving creek, where boys of all ages idle along the quay in all weathers, waiting for the tide to fill the basin enough for them to jump, shrieking and whooping, into the muddy water.

Anxious to have something to write about the town, a hungry Samuel Ireland wanders into the churchyard where he was . . . *enabled at least to feed the imagination with a whimsical allusion to the different stages of our 'strange eventful history'.*

*Our life is nothing but a winter's day,*
*Some only break their fast, and so away;*
*Others stay to dinner, and depart full fed,*
*The deepest age but sups, and goes to bed.*
*He's most in debt that lingers out the day,*
*Who dies by times, has less and less to pay.*

A rather pecuniary ditty, no longer in evidence in the churchyard, (if indeed it ever was) but understandably one that the hungry would linger over. For the well-fed, a more optimistic epitaph among the fascinating array of tombstones, reads:

Grieve not for me my husband dear
I am not lost , but sleeping here.
My grave is made, my bed you see,
Prepare along to follow me.

*The old 'Radio Caroline' off Queenborough*

# Cooling Castle

*This noble ruin stands about the centre of the hundred of Hoo, and, from its situation, was intended as a defence both for the river Thames and Medway, being placed nearly at equal distances from each.*

Cooling Castle impressed Ireland enough for him to *digress from the bank of the Medway* for three miles and sketch this *noble ruin* which stands in the centre of the Hoo Peninsula, midway between the rivers Thames and Medway. Standing among trees on flat land, surrounded by farm buildings, it is hardly noticeable from a distance. The minor road sweeps the unsuspecting motorist past the perfectly preserved gatehouse, where the traveller is momentarily dwarfed by a child's storybook castle, with machicolated chunky towers, crowning the pie-crust rim of two perfect roundels. A speedy flashback to the Age of Chivalry and intrigue, where the following inscription, dating from the 15th century, can still be read and is visible in Ireland's sketch:

> . . . made in help of the countre;
> In knowing of which thing
> This is chartre, and witnessing.

These strange words were to show that the 3rd Earl of Cobham, who built the castle in 1381, did so to defend his country from French and Spanish after they had dispatched a force up the Thames in 1379, burning unprotected villages and stealing cattle. Richard II then gave the earl his permission to turn his manor house at Cooling into what was possibly the last genuine castle to be built in England. It is also reputed to be the first designed for use of hand-held firearms, which the architect Yvele had heard about from China, but were not used in England for another seventy years.

In the 18th century, the moat was choked and the walls ivy-clad, but now, cleared and cleaned, it gives a mirror image of the ancient castle amongst the reeds and flags. Today, the slit-eyed walls of this ruined giant rise gently from a field of new-mown grass. Even the willow in Ireland's sketch still weeps graciously upon this stage of history. In the 14th century, Lord Cobham (Sir John Oldcastle) championed the Lollards, a body of religious reformers, and held the castle in a six-hour inglorious siege during Wyatt's Rebellion. Oldcastle was a friend of Prince Hal (later Henry V), and Shakespeare, believing him to have led the young prince astray, portrayed Sir John Oldcastle as his lawless and greedy knight, Sir John Falstaff, in his play, *Henry V*. This was such an unjust slight on Oldcastle's character that Shakespeare had to apologise; in the epilogue of *Henry V* Part 2, Shakespeare says of Falstaff: 'Oldcastle died a martyr, and this is not the man.'

Empathising with Lord Cobham, Ireland writes:

*intrepid Sir John, whose courage was equalled but by his piety and goodness of heart; qualities that were fully evinced by his warm espousal of the doctrine of Wickliff, against the bigotry and tyranny of the church of Rome.*

Walking through the massive gatehouse, Ireland was happy to note that,

*a very comfortable farm house is now standing within these desolated walls, where industry and useful labour are promoted, and more beneficial effects derived to the state, than ever arose from the splendor and warlike pride of any feudal barony.*

This house was built by Sir Thomas Whitmore in 1650 on the site of the old Saxon manor.

At the close of the 20th century, the scene is similarly peaceful; only birdsong and the occasional car disturb the silence. The original owner, Sir John Oldcastle, might be amused to know that his residence has now been given licence as a venue for civil weddings, and is used for corporate functions and private parties.

For all this domesticity, walking the Hoo Peninsula on a windy day conjures up Dickens's novel, *Great Expectations,* in which he gives a graphic and chilling account of the dark, flat wilderness of the marshes, where, ' . . . the river was a low leaden line, and the sea a distant savage lair.' In Dickens's horizontal grey-scape the only vertical things seen were a beacon and a gibbet. It was the perfect setting for convicts, pirates, and smugglers to do their worst. In the churchyard at Cooling five little stone lozenges, where Pip's brothers were supposedly buried, are still visible.

# Gillingham

*... the village of Gillingham ... claims, from its elevated situation, particular attention. On the force of antiquity it likewise merits notice.*

Today, Gillingham, the largest of the Medway towns, could hardly be described as a village. It is hard enough for the curious traveller to find the parish church among the profusion of Victorian terraced houses, Chinese takeaways and fish and chip shops stacked up the hill. An inauspicious road leads to the beautiful 14th century parish church of St Mary Magdalene, sitting calmly on Gillingham Green. This welcome open space gives a good view over an empty Gillingham Reach, with Hoo Fort on its saltmarsh and Kingsnorth power-station beyond. Not quite the scene Ireland describes two hundred years ago:

*From the church yard the view is beautiful and extensive, comprising a rich and fertile country, with the winding Medway beneath, and in the distance a noble expansive view of the ocean, bearing its stately burthens.*

After the Norman Conquest, Gillingham was owned by the Archbishops of Canterbury who built a palace here in the 12th century. According to Ireland, *The manor formerly belonged to the Archbishops of Canterbury, who had a stately palace; part of it is still remaining, and serves as an excellent barn.*

Gillingham Church would have been the chapel for this palace but, as Gillingham grew in importance in the 14th century, the church was enlarged, and a fair and market were held regularly on the green. The Archbishop's Palace was suppressed by Henry VIII, and the church was rid of *the miraculous lady of Gillingham*, which is evidently a great relief to the staunchly Protestant Samuel Ireland: *The niche still remains; but the good lady, with her train of idolaters, and her trade of miracles, thank heaven, no longer flourish on this coast!*

The church may well have been in decline when Ireland visited it at the end of the 18th century. He mentions the 14th and 15th century monuments to the influential Beaufitz family, which must then have been in a state of disrepair, for he tells us: *the records of whose military prowess and politics are now, from time and neglect, scarcely understood.*

Now, the monuments have vanished without trace; but records survive, giving the information that would once have been legible on the monuments. At least one member of the Beaufitz family had been a shipowner, whilst another accompanied Richard II on his expedition to Ireland. The parish register also tells us that, in 1667, the year of the Dutch invasion, a number of soldiers were buried in the churchyard, as well as French prisoners who had been detained on hulks during the Napoleonic Wars.

Ireland fails to mention the copper Norman font, arcaded with 16 bays, covered with an old oak canopy. In his time, the church was falling into disrepair, and during major restoration work in the 19th century, the priceless font was found outside being used as a cattle trough. Strangely, Ireland does not mention the famous Will Adams, who was baptised in Gillingham Church, and whose story of the discovery of Japan in the early part of the 17th century has been immortalised in the film *Shogun*. A stone clock tower in Watling Street, Gillingham, built in 1934, makes a more tangible memorial to the 'blue-eyed Samurai'.

A visitor today would find the church in good order. Its restored interior shines with white paint and tender loving care, and the old font is again used for baptisms. Arthur Mee, in his *King's England Series on Kent,* dismisses Gillingham in two scathing sentences: 'It is the biggest and least characteristic town in Kent. Its chief possessions are a font of one church and the ruins of another.'

One of the oldest man-made artefacts along the Medway is a fragment of Greek sculpture in St Mary's Church, Chatham, now The Medway Heritage Centre. A carved relief on stone, it is the headless but still beautiful figure of Euphrosyne, one of the Three Graces. She sits in the church porch like a graceful pauper, her left hand raised, pointing to the future with a finger of the right hand. With his love of classical antiquity, Samuel Ireland would certainly have mentioned this figure if it had been there. It was found embedded in the wall of the Norman chapel when this part of the church was demolished.

Opposite the church stands a bronze equestrian statue of Lord Kitchener which was removed from Khartoum and brought to Chatham in 1961, the year of Sudan's independence. Lord Kitchener was commissioned into the Royal Engineers in 1871.

Gordon of Khartoum, another Royal Engineer, sits defiantly on his camel, gazing out across a much-changed Medway inside the barracks grounds.

Although he has no statue here, Charles Dickens lived at No. 11 Ordnance Terrace from 1817 to 1821. His father, John, was in the Pay Office of Chatham dockyard after his transfer from Portsmouth. Later, financial difficulties forced them to move down-market to The Brook, Chatham.

# Brompton

*The village of Brompton is happily situated for the purposes to which it is applied; its wholesome air, and easy ascent from Chatham, rendering every accommodation for the use of the mariners and soldiery that occupy the barracks so judiciously erected there. The view from hence is rich and extensive; it comprizes the river Thames in the distance, a fertile and varied combination of objects composed of hills and dales, oatlands and hop-grounds, together with the meandring of the Medway beneath.*

Two hundred years on, ascending the hill from Chatham past the Royal School of Military Engineering, the cramped streets are lined with serried ranks of workers' houses. An occasional 18th century building leans against 19th and 20th century counterparts, and there is nothing happy about it. However, on reaching the summit, Mr Ireland would at last have felt at home. The village retains some green spaces and many of its 18th century buildings, including a well-preserved terrace called Prospect Row. From the third-storey windows of these elegant homes, the view over an industrial Medway would be visible, but at ground level, housing estates and flats cascade down the hill, giving only tantalising glimpses of the river curving beneath. Ireland must have had good eyesight to see the Thames, and the view today is certainly less *rich and extensive*. Metal warehouses, cranes, gasometers and close-packed houses replace the *oatlands and hop-grounds*. The highest part of the Downs is still visible on the horizon above the houses. As always, history lives on in the names: Garrison Church, The Cannon Pub, Khartoum Road, and Amhurst Redoubt show the strategic importance of this vantage point. Ireland would have been happy to know that the monarchs and politicians of the 19th century took the defence of their country seriously.

*A glimpse of Brompton*

# Upnor Castle

*A pleasing object of the picturesque kind . . . but, as a place of national defence, I fear has never answered any purpose whatever; yet it must be allowed to have its merits as a place of snug security for a governor, storekeeper, clerk of the cheque etc. The governor has the command of all the forts on the river except Sheerness.*

This castle lies two-thirds of the way down Chatham Reach and has changed little since Ireland made these rather unfair comments. According to Samuel Pepys, Upnor acquitted itself well during the Dutch raid of June 1667. He wrote in his famous diary, 'I do not see that Upnor Castle hath received any hurt by them though they played long against it; and they themselves shot till they had hardly a gun left upon the carriages, so badly provided they were.' It was lack of munitions, not courage, that was Upnor's failing.

Upnor Castle faces the river and is best seen from the water. It is indeed a *picturesque* 16th century fort, built by Queen Elizabeth I in 1561 when the Armada threat led to greater security of the river and the inception of Chatham dockyard. A long, rectangular building, with round towers at each end, and integral tube-like turrets, it sits on the waterfront, cloaked in trees, like a defiant Elizabethan courtier, spreading a defensive triangle of wooden palisades into the water. The mellow stone is said to come from the outer walls of Rochester Castle. Upnor is a snapshot from the past, juxtaposed with the 20th century industrial and dockyard landscape of the opposite bank. Surrounded by modern houses, pubs and marinas, it takes the onlooker by surprise.

After the Dutch attack on the Medway in the 17th century, Upnor was considered useless as a fort for defence, but became a 'Place of Stores and Magazine'. In 1827, it was fitted up as an Ordnance Laboratory, and later used as Armament Stores for the Navy. In 1891, Upnor and its depot were transferred from the War Office to the Admiralty, and the Naval Armament Supply Department was formed. After serving as part of the Magazine Establishment during the Second World War, and sustaining damage by two bombs which fell in the garden of Upnor House in 1941, it has finally been 'demobbed'. The castle is now a national monument cared for by English Heritage and open to the public.

History lives on in unexpected ways. A cannon ball, fired by the Dutch during Admiral de Ruyter's attack upon Upnor Castle in June 1667, was removed from the beach below the castle in 1960. In 1962, it was presented to the Royal Netherlands Yacht Club by a group of Upnor yachtsmen and now serves as the trophy for the annual competition of ocean-racing yachts between the Dutch and the English. Samuel Ireland, Esq. would no doubt, have found this story a little perplexing.

It was fortunate for our 18th century artist that Upnor had no mounted guns. While sketching the castle, *peacefully situated beneath the stern of a man-of-war, to keep under the wind, he was visited by a person from on board, who claimed the privilege of taking him before the Commissioner in Chatham yard, to answer for his rash attempt on this noble place of defence.*

Having successfully persuaded the Commissioner that, *he had no insidious design against the navy, or the welfare of his country, he was suffered to depart in peace; and that he might not again be taken into custody for similar offences, the Commissioner politely furnished him with a passport, of which the following is a copy:*

*To the officers of his Majesty's ships in ordinary.*

*SAMUEL IRELAND, Esq. of Norfolk Street, London, may be allowed to amuse himself by taking views.'*

*August 25th, 1791. C. PROBY.*

This very *Commissioner in Chatham Yard* is buried in a vault in St Mary's Church, Chatham, now a Heritage Centre. A memorial plaque on the wall tells us that, Commissioner Charles Proby died on 31 March 1799 and his son, Charles Proby Cunningham, a midshipman, died in 1822 aged twenty years.

Safe now in his little craft, tucked under the stern of one of His Majesty's men-of-war, Samuel Ireland looked downstream with satisfaction:

*. . . the easy bend of the river, with the luxuriant scenery of its woody banks, and receding distant hills, make a beautiful combination of objects in picturesque landscape.*

At the end of the 20th century, the same retrospective view would be a little less picturesque. On the other bank of the river, Chatham's dockyard spills into an industrial wasteland; brick warehouses, metal sheds, cranes, gasworks, and factory chimneys line the *easy bend*. Men-of-war, fishing boats and barges have been replaced by pleasure craft. Now motorboats, graceful yachts, bright-sailed dinghies and paddle-steamers liven up the river. Yacht clubs sprout along the banks of Chatham and Gillingham Reaches. Masts congregate like matchsticks below the wooded hills, safe behind marina palisades. Bright buoys mark the navigable channels, and moored yachts bead the river, where sinister hulks once lined the watery fairway.

Just below the castle, close to the shore, *is affixed a stone denoting the boundary of the city's jurisdiction upon the river. Its ancient date is 1204, and on it is inscribed 'God preserve the city of London'. The present stone was erected in 1771, in the mayoralty of Brass Crosby Esq.*

Today, the 1771 stone sits uncomfortably on an extended pavement near the Medway Yacht Club, looking like a misshapen bollard, dwarfed by an elegant granite stone erected in 1836. The inscription mentioned by Ireland on the old stone is still clearly visible, though most of the lettering beneath is illegible. The strong black lettering on the 19th century stone announces: *Right Hon. Willm Taylor Copeland Lord Mayor, John Lainson Esq. and David Salomons Esq. Sheriffs. Sir John Pirie Bart 1842, and Sir James Duke, 1849.* Sir David Salomon's nephew became mayor of Tunbridge Wells in 1894-5, inheriting his uncle's estates at Broomhill as well as his brains, energy and entrepreneurial skills.

As far back as 1204, the Lord Mayor and Corporation of the City of London claimed certain rights, particularly of fishing, over the waters of the Lower Medway. There is a mark known as the London Stone at the Thames mouth of Yantlet Creek, as well as this one at Upnor and another near Burham known as the Hawkwood Stone. This curious monument sits behind railings on the reedy marshland like a lonely tomb. The simple 18th century pillar has been mounted on an ornate base, added in 1864, giving more room for the mayors to receive immortality. The inscription states: *This stone was erected at the Admiralty Court holden for the Mayor and Cityzens on the 19th day of July 1799 in the Mayorality of William Prentice Esqe.* On the rear of the pillar is an inscription dated 1864: *God Preserve the City of Rochester.* These stones record the mayor's jurisdiction over an area within the City, from Sheerness to Hawkwood, a distance of eighteen miles. The preservation of the correct boundary lines was extremely important for, going back as far as the 16th century, each mayor had to 'beat the bounds' with some of his citizens as part of his civic duties. If he neglected this perambulation, on horseback or on foot, every mayor had to pay a fine of £5.00, a hefty sum in 1591.

*Gazebo in Upnor*

# Chatham

*We now approach Chatham, whose royal dock yard, fortifications, and repository for naval stores and ordnance, at once fill the mind with the most pleasing sensation of the happy security , and prudent defence of our country.*

Samuel Ireland's prose here glows with patriotic pride, as well it might for the dockyard started from small beginnings. In 1547, at the end of Henry VIII's reign, a building was rented in Gillingham Water for the storage of rigging and sails, belonging to the royal ships then wintering in the Medway. From this one building, rented for 13 shillings and sixpence, grew the country's premier dockyard, whose fortunes ebbed and flowed with war and peace for the next 400 years.

Gradually, more land and buildings were acquired and a mast pond was completed in 1570. In these early years, most of the work undertaken was connected with the maintenance and repair of royal ships. It was not until 1586 that Chatham built its first vessel, a 40-ton pinnace named *Sunne* which left the Medway with the Fleet, sailing west to join Sir Francis Drake at Plymouth to engage the Spanish Armada. The dockyard continued to expand rapidly, and by 1699 covered 68 acres and employed 900 workers, the largest civilian employer in the country.

The store house and wharf, usually called the Old Dock, which is situated on a slip of land below the chalk cliff, between the church and the river, was the original dockyard until King James, in 1622, finding it too small for the growing service of the navy, removed it to the present spot.

Theoretically, the dockyard was ideally placed to make ships, at anchor in the Medway, ready to take offensive action if required. In 1667, when the Dutch invaded, the Navy was, however, unprepared as Ireland describes.

*Charles I, greatly improved his father's plan, enlarged the site of the yard, and made new docks for floating ships in with the tide. Charles II, likewise, often talked of making farther improvements, and visited this place with that intention; but having viewed the Royal Sovereign, and passed a few joyous hours in the neighbourhood, thought no more of the navy or dock, till Admiral De Ruyter, about seven years after, reminded him of his neglected duty, and their defenceless state.*

The lesson was learnt the hard way and, as a result, Chatham dockyard grew and flourished. In 1793 Ireland writes:

*The present naval dock ranges along the eastern bank of the river for near a mile in length; the improvements and additional buildings it has received within a few years are astonishing . . . a first rate man-of-war has often been equipped for sea in a few weeks . . . in times of war the persons employed in and about this yard exceed three thousand.*

As he continues, his enthusiasm mounts:

*The royal wharf, in which the guns belonging to the shipping in the river are deposited, the huge pyramids of cannon balls, and vast range of storehouse, in which are deposited every species of hostile weapons, one would suppose need only to be shewn to the enemy, to intimidate them from an attack.*

England's legendary victory over the Spanish Armada left a legacy of wounded and disabled seamen, to whom the nation seemed totally indifferent. Their plight was so great that it stirred Sir Francis Drake and Sir John Hawkins to inaugurate a special fund to provide for mariners and shipwrights in need. Ireland proudly informs us:

*The noble fund established under the appellation of The Chest at Chatham, was instituted in 1588, . . . when every man voluntarily assigned a portion of his pay to the succour of his wounded fellow. The institution was sanctioned by Queen Elizabeth and has continued ever since.*

What he does not tell us is that this fund was frequently abused by unscrupulous administrators and, in the 17th century, theft, looting and embezzlement were commonplace in the dockyard.

Flourishing though it was, Chatham was being superseded by Portsmouth by the end of the 17th century. In the 18th century, the French were replacing the Dutch as Britain's major enemy, so Portsmouth was more strategically placed, and the waters of the Medway were beginning to shoal. Although fewer ships were sent for refitting, Chatham continued to build new ships for the Navy during the 18th century, the most famous of these being *The Victory,* Nelson's flagship.

By the mid-19th century, there was a renewal of activity and, between 1862 and 1865, the dockyard was extended, quadrupling the area occupied in Ireland's time. The new facilities included four dry-docks, factory buildings, hydraulic capstans and numerous steam-cranes. The centrepiece was three interlinked basins running the length of the former St Mary's Creek and designed for receiving warships. Hundreds of convicts helped with the hard labour required for this ambitious extension, and a prison was built on the site to accommodate them. Gradually, the wooden walls of the men-of-war, that Ireland speaks of with such pride and affection, were being replaced by ironclad steamships such as the battleship, *Achilles*, built at Chatham in the 1860s.

The first half of the 20th century kept Chatham dockyard busy with two World Wars, when battleships, destroyers, cruisers, sloops and submarines were built. There was unemployment again between the wars, but the building of the 5,500 ton cruiser, *Arethusa,* and the Oberon class of submarines helped to keep the dockyard going. There was frenetic activity again during the Second World War and, in 1940, when an air-raid threatened the dockyard, the *Arethusa* opened fire with her anti-aircraft guns while in dry-dock.

The post-war years brought decline. In 1962, the submarine, *Ocelot,* was the last warship built for the Royal Navy at Chatham, and has been preserved as a tourist attraction. Rumours of closure were only silenced when it was announced that Chatham would be the site of a multi-million pound nuclear refit centre. It was to be a short reprieve and, in June 1981, the proposed closure of the dockyard was announced in the House of Commons. On 1 April 1984, the former naval dockyard came into the possession of three separate bodies: Chatham Historic Dockyard Trust, English Estates and the Medway Dock Company. After a lot of repair and restoration, the Historic Dockyard has become a living museum where, with the help of audiovisual displays and life-size mannequins, the visitor can recapture a little of the

Plate V

Chatham

Plate VI

Rochester from Frindsbury Hill

Plate VII

Temple Farm, Strood

Plate VIII

Lord Darnley's Mausoleum at Cobham Park

romance of the days when the wooden walls of the great men-of-war defended our country and colonised many parts of the world, changing the course of history.

For all this technical gloss, there is a haunting emptiness here. From the well-tended Commissioner's garden, to the slack machines in the rope-houses, the empty boards of the vast mould-loft, and the bare chapel, there echoes a silent resonance, all the more potent because this is an authentic stage. As visitors leave the pristine covered slips, sealed at the river's edge, they look across empty water at an incontinent sprawl of buildings and industry. Where the area has been cleared for new buildings, the green slit eyes of Legoland flats and offices wink across the water. Dead leaves rustle on the concrete where once hundreds of pairs of feet went about their business, planning, drawing, sawing, caulking, sewing, spinning, hammering. An empty stage on which so many livelihoods once depended; where comedies, tragedies, victories and defeats were played out over four centuries. The Medway, once filled with the masts of men-of-war, fishing boats, barges and sailing ships, today slides quietly by, just a broad band of ghost-filled empty water.

*Old paddle-tug at Chatham*

Alongside the slips where Nelson's *Victory,* the first major ironship *Achilles,* and many other warships were launched, the last paddle-steamer tug perches amongst the weeds, crippled and rusting. Another paddle-steamer, the *Medway Queen,* is currently in an equally sorry state. Built in 1924, she was a pleasure-steamer on the estuary until the outbreak of the Second World War when she was called up to serve King and country. She evacuated children from Kent at the start of the war, rescued 7,000 allied troops from Dunkirk and, when refitted as a minesweeper, shot down three enemy aircraft. Since then she has been saved from the ship-breaker's yard, served as a clubhouse, and sunk no fewer than three times, most recently on New Year's Eve 1997 near her berth at Kingsnorth Power Station. Dragged from her muddy grave yet again, her ongoing life now depends on the enthusiasm and goodwill of the Preservation Society who own her. Ironically, it is a similar paddle-steamer, the *Kingswear Castle,* from Dartmouth, which now carries tourists up and down the Medway.

*The P.S. Kingswear Castle*

However, the river here does not only look back. Mr Ireland might be interested to see the great Lloyds Marine Insurance building lying beside the Chatham ropery. Edward Lloyd started this prestigious company in a coffee-house in 17th century London and, in 1972, it was relocated at Gun Wharf, Chatham. Just down river, on the south bank, 350 acres of former dockland, including St Mary's Island, are rapidly metamorphosing into a 21st century social supermarket catering for every living, working and leisure need.

Rumour has it, that since the Napoleonic Wars, there has been a troubled spirit in St Mary's Barracks, Chatham. Ghost stories abound and the following anecdote was passed on by a naval officer who spent many years of his working life in Chatham. At the end of the 18th century, a guard at the barracks went to sleep while on duty. He and his mate were guarding some French prisoners of war. Sleeping on duty was a serious offence, but the second guard went off duty without waking his comrade. During the night, a French prisoner grabbed the sleeping guard's bayonet and killed him with it.

Nearly 200 years later, two naval stokers were given a night's accommodation in the large empty dormitory of the little-used barracks. The two men chose to sleep in beds at opposite ends of the room. During the night, one of the men was roughly shaken awake, and his bedding ripped off. He leapt out of bed in a fury, thinking the other man had done this. Shouting and cursing at each other, the two stokers soon came to blows and, as fighting was a punishable offence, they were hauled up before the Naval Barracks Commander.

The puzzled stokers were let off lightly with a caution. It transpired that the ghost of the guard, who left his sleeping comrade to be attacked and killed by a French prisoner, was known to rudely awaken seamen who slept in this room. His guilt could not let him rest in peace.

*A Thames barge*

# Rochester from Frindsbury Hill

*We now approach the venerable city of Rochester, which, in point of antiquity, is inferior to few in the kingdom, having been founded as early as the year 43, when Plautus came into Britain. Justus, one of the missionaries who came over with Augustine to convert the Saxons, was his first bishop.*

Such a cavalcade of famous people have crossed Rochester Bridge on their way to this *venerable city*, that past is fused with present. The castle and cathedral, monumental survivors of a turbulent history, are now cleaned and restored to welcome visitors. Great and notorious prelates include Paulinus, Rochester's first bishop, Gundulf who was responsible for building not only most of the cathedral, but also the castle keep, John Fisher who lost his head on Tower Hill in 1535 and Nicholas Ridley who was burned as a heretic in 1555.

Royal visitors, from King Ethelred to Queen Victoria, have passed this way. Henry VIII met Anne of Cleves in Rochester, Charles II, at his Restoration, spent the night here in Restoration House; James II fled to France via the Medway, through the back garden of Abdication House. Artistic and literary figures have enjoyed themselves in Rochester. William Hogarth played hopscotch outside the Guildhall, and Samuel Pepys climbed up the castle keep with 'three pretty maids'. Charles Dickens has immortalised the city in his novels, and his last unfinished work, *Edwin Drood*, was set around the cathedral.

On foot, from Frindsbury Hill across Rochester Bridge is the best way to enter the city and, with a lot of mental subtraction, re-enter the past. A narrow tarmac path buried beneath high fences hides a sea of metal warehouses on the left, while on the right, a quarried chalk escarpment shelves steeply down from the churchyard. To the west, Strood sprawls across the gently rising hillside, a jumbled web of terraced houses, light industry, superstores, car parks and railway bridges. Across the bare stretch of water, two glaring gasometers mark the point where the river curves sharply into Limehouse Reach. A boat repair yard lies on the east bank, where the roof tops of greater Rochester form a backdrop to the old city's cathedral and castle.

*A conglomeration in Limehouse Reach*

Upstream, the view is dominated by the M2 bridge, opened on 29 May 1963. This delicate strand of concrete, balanced on graceful pillars, soars above the Medway, making the 1914 ferro-concrete bridge at Rochester look like an antediluvian relative in a steel corset. Planning permission is currently being sought for a further bridge to carry the Channel Tunnel Rail Link. Blue and white motorboats, like so many buoys, line the river beneath the castle walls, leaving what was once known as the 'city of barges' with a strangely empty waterway.

*The M2 motorway bridge from Cuxton*

Dickens describes Rochester High Street in the middle of the 19th century as silent and 'full of gables with old beams . . . oddly garnished with a queer old clock that projects over the pavement out of a grave, red building, as if Time carried on business there and hung out his sign.'

Today, pristine Georgian houses border the tidy streets, the old clock still projects over the pavement, and Dickens lives on in Peggoty's Parlour, A Taste of Two Cities, and Edwin Drood's house. Shorts Reach, below Borstal village, once the home of the famous Shorts seaplanes, is now called The Esplanade. It has been revitalised with smart warehouse-style apartments, and pays homage to Rochester's most famous author with names like Oliver Twist, Magwitch and Tupman. For this city, the way forward is to look back; Chatham dockyard rings to the sound of heritage boat-building, Fort Amhurst echoes bugle and drum, while The Dickens Centre makes fact of fiction. In the 1990s, Rochester is indeed the city of 'Great Expectations.'

The Romans built the first bridge over the Medway here, and Rochester became an important Roman station, situated as it was on the main road of Watling Street, which ran from Dover through London to Chester. This Roman masonry bridge lasted until 960 A.D. when it was rebuilt in timber by the Saxons. Fires, floods and ice damaged this bridge so much that, in 1293, people had to cross the river in boats. Repair costs nearly bankrupted many of the landowners responsible for the upkeep of the piers. Finally, in 1392, it was replaced by a substantial stone bridge which lasted until 1856. The present bridge was completed in 1916 and today is really three bridges, one rail and two road.

In 1793, Samuel Ireland describes the

*ancient gothic bridge . . . built of stone, and consists of eleven pointed arches, supported by substantial piers . . . in length 566 feet, but in breadth only 14, a space so confined and narrow as to render the passage, more than incommodious, from the great traffic carrying on here.*

Two hundred years later, nothing seems to have changed, as cars crawl, bumper-to-bumper over the two dual carriageway bridges. Ireland also comments favourably on the strength of the medieval bridge, remarking that *the body of water that falls through the arches flows with a torrent and rapidity equal to any thing I remember to have noticed.* It seems remarkable that a bridge, built in the 14th century, could have lasted nearly 500 years.

In 1489, the Archbishop of Canterbury, John Morton, described sarcastically by Ireland as *this delight of heaven,* endeavoured to raise money by a different method:

*He did not hesitate to publish a remission of sins for forty days to all such persons who would contribute any thing towards the repair of this very useful, if not pious work. It would have been creditable to the Roman Catholic faith if the pecuniary advantages arising from absolution had never been worse applied! To these repentant sinners it is that the bridge owes part of its coping and iron railing.*

These iron railings had their uses, as was observed in 1641 by the French Ambassador, The Marquis de la Ferte-Imbaut:

'The country is beautiful, especially near the large village of Rochester, which is chiefly observable on account of its bridge, furnished with high iron railings, that drunkards, not uncommon here, may not mix water with their wine.'

Some traditions live on, and Rochester Bridge is still administered by the Bridge Trust, a charity which pays for its upkeep.

Of Rochester Castle, Ireland notes:

*It is now supposed to be seven hundred years since the building of Rochester castle . . . It is certainly well situated to guard the important pass over the Medway; and from the defence it has frequently made during the conflicts between the Barons and the Kings of England, may justly be considered as having been a place of considerable strength.*

It is 900 years since the castle was first built in 1086, at the time of the Norman Conquest, and was rebuilt for William Rufus, after the death of William the Conqueror, by Gundulf, Bishop of Rochester. The keep, which we see today, was added in 1127. Ireland takes up the story:

*The castle was, in the time of William the Conqueror, in the custody of his bastard brother Odo, Bishop of Baieux, a turbulent prelate, who, after the death of his sovereign, raised an insurrection in the county of Kent.*

Before the *turbulent* prelate was disgraced, he was made Earl of Kent and *destroyed and pillaged many places.* Dismayed when Normandy was separated from England after the Conqueror's death, he and a group of like-minded Norman barons made Rochester a rebel stronghold and caused the first siege of Rochester in 1088. William Rufus, besieged the city which was compelled to surrender. Odo lost his lands and privileges and was imprisoned in Tonbridge Castle before he returned to Normandy. The king then strengthened Rochester Castle and asked Bishop Gundulf, who was responsible for building the Tower of London, to execute the work for him at his own expense.

The *Textus Roffensis,* an early 12th century register of Rochester Cathedral Priory, painstakingly records the intrigues between church and state in these unruly times. Samuel Ireland tells us that this . . . *curious manuscript . . . was lost for some considerable time, during the troubles in the last century, and was very near being irrecoverably so in the present, having been borrowed by Doctor Harris, for the use of his intended history of this county. It was forwarded to London in a vessel which was overset in its passage, and the book lay for several hours under water, by which accident it received considerable damage.*

The massive keep, known as Gundulf's Tower, still stands guard over this strategic river crossing like a proud old soldier defiantly protecting the bridge. A stone's-throw away, the well-preserved cathedral has been a sign of Christian worship since Saxon times. These two buildings, encapsulating the history of Rochester, rise above the city like two eminences grises.

*This tower, is so conspicuous an object as to be discernible at a distance of twenty miles; and from its summit we command a grand and extensive prospect of the river Medway, comprizing views both above and below the bridge, even to its conflux with the Thames.*

Samuel Ireland's description is less valid today, as the omnipresent power-station at Kingsnorth dwarfs the estuary like a giant beanstalk, and interrupts the view to the mouth of the Medway.

On the subject of the castle our 18th century artist adds an interesting rider:

*Divers lands in this and other counties are held of this castle, the tenures of which are perfect castle guard; for every tenant who does not duly discharge his proper rent, suit and services, is liable to have it doubled on the return of every tide of the Medway, during the time it remains unpaid, according to the ancient custom of this manor. On St Andrew's day, old style, the ceremony of hanging out a banner at the house of the receiver of the rents is still preserved.*

To the west of Boley Hill, near Rochester Castle, lies the elegant Georgian mansion of the 16th century M.P., Mr Richard Watts. This remarkable gentleman was not only prominent in city affairs, a former mayor and founder of almshouses, he was also responsible for the day-to-day running of Upnor Castle. Not surprisingly, therefore, he had the honour of entertaining his queen, Elizabeth I, on her return from an excursion round the counties of Kent and Sussex in 1573, a worrying experience for any host, as Ireland recounts:

*At her departure, her host making an apology for his house, as being too small and humble for the reception of a royal guest, the Queen, looking round, expressed her full approbation of the place and manner in which she had been received, by the Latin word SATIS, since which time the house has borne that appelation.*

Richard Watts, M.P., is also remembered for his philanthropy. A substantial gabled house in the High Street bears the following inscription:

That any six poor travellers, not rogues or proctors, may here receive gratis, for one night, lodging, entertainment, and four-pence each.

Ireland uses the theory, offered by the Reverend S. Denne in 1772, to explain why proctors and rogues *became coupled in this good man's interdiction.*

Mr Watts, in poor health, employed a proctor to make a will. The wily man decided that charity begins at home . . . *perverted his employer's benevolent intention, and gave to himself that which was dedicated to God and to pious uses. Upon detection of this fraud, the testator appears to have been earnest to transmit to posterity, in the style and description of his charity, the character and profession of the miscreant, who had in this manner attempted to abuse his trust.*

However, as proctors were lawfully appointed by lepers and bedridden people to collect charitable alms for them, and were generally equated with the idea of a rogue, this seems reason enough to exclude them from his free lodgings. *The sum bequeathed for the annual support of this charity in 1570, amounted to thirty-six pounds, which estate now produces a nett yearly income of five hundred.*

Whatever the reason, the house is now a tourist attraction and, simply furnished for weary 16th century travellers, is on view for the 20th century tourist.

Ireland now explores the *venerable gothic cathedral of Rochester.* He expresses pleasure that the thick coats of plaster were being removed from the pillars to expose the Petworth marble beneath, and adds obsequiously . . . *Much praise is due to the Dean and Chapter of this cathedral, who have, with such laudable respect and taste, evinced their zeal for the preservation of the gothic beauties of this venerable structure.*

It would seem from Ireland's comments that a whiff of Puritanism still hung in the air at the end of the 18th century . . . *The good sense of the present day is likewise shown in the new regulations which have taken place in the collegiate body: they have enabled the Chapter to make a valuable addition to their library, by calling upon every member, dean, prebendary, at the time of his admission, to apply a sum of money in the purchase of books, instead of wasting it in a costly entertainment.*

Much praise is still due to the Dean and Chapter, for Rochester Cathedral has been recently cleaned and the mellow stones of the west front gleam in a magnificent, if slightly broken, smile. This fine Romanesque facade, with four pointed turrets, deeply corrugated with slim pillars and decorated arcades, soars upwards to balance its great width. Dickens, through his character Mr Grewgious in *Edwin Drood*, describes a peep into the cathedral as 'looking down the throat of Old Time'. The interior is a joyful amalgam of sturdy Norman and delicate Gothic architecture. Bold piecrust arcades and chunky pillars blend easily with the delicate Gothic arches of new-found wealth and confidence. After 900 years of turbulent history, when the cathedral suffered pillage, fires and desecration, it has emerged weathered, but not beaten, leaving a quiet and holy space in our frenetic world.

*A corner of Rochester*

# Frindsbury

*The village of Frindsbury is situated on an eminence which commands an extensive and noble prospect of the Medway, Rochester bridge, castle, and town, with the hills of Kent giving a rich and beautiful distance. Frindsbury is of great antiquity.*

The eminence to which Ireland refers is known as the Frindsbury peninsula. Once a gently sloping area of fields and orchards, years of quarrying have produced a sheer wall of chalk, topped with trees and crowned by Frindsbury Church. Ireland does not describe the 11th century church in any detail, but merely quotes from the following inscription which obviously amused him:

*All Saints' Church, Frindsbury*

*A list of sundry pious persons, who, loving this place, have left the following benefactions to the poor.*

*There is not a single name of a benefactor upon the stone; but at the bottom is written, to certify this lack of charity,*

*"Witness our hands,*

*William Gibbons, Vicar".*

Fifty years earlier, Hogarth and friends discovered the same inscription on their *Peregrination into Kent* in 1732. Having proceeded *Merrily to Frendsbury* they write:

'We there reviewed the church and churchyard, pleasantly situated. There were some bad epitaphs, and in the church is hung up a list of benefactions to the parish, at the bottom of which is wrote "Witness our Hands" and is subscribed with the name of William Gibbons only. This seems a little odd, but being in such a place, we imagined there might be some mystery to it, so enquired no further.'

There is no sign of the inscription in the church today, but major restoration work was undertaken in the 19th century, and the church interior liberally doused with whitewash. Nor is there any trace of William Gibbons in the long list of incumbents in the porch. Whatever changes have occurred, the building itself is a notable landmark. Perched high on its shrinking cliffside churchyard, it still boasts one of the best views of the river and the burgeoning Medway towns.

What Ireland did not know in 1793 was that the bones of a giant elephant lay beneath this eminence until 1911, when the Royal Engineers, digging a trench beside the hard at Upnor, found them. They did not appreciate the importance of their find, and it was left to a Mr S. Turner, searching for flints in the area a few years later, to bring the bones to the attention of the Natural History Museum, London. They were then painstakingly excavated, and all 3.8 metres of Upnor elephant (Palaeoloxodon Antiquos) now stands in that museum.

In 1925, seventeen heaps of flints were discovered near All Saints' Church, during an excavation of the chalk. The find amounted to some 4,000 stone tools and weapons. These artefacts were shaped by the hand of man around 100,000 BC and left by the banks of the ancient Medway, eventually to be covered by the flood loam of the river.

Ireland has his own story to tell regarding discoveries here:

*In digging within this cliff there has been recently discovered at a distance of fifteen or sixteen feet from the surface, a leaden coffin in the ancient circular form, with a cross on one side, and a number of figures indented thereon in the form of large cockle shells. The coffin was broken to pieces in digging it out; but within it was found a small vessel about seven inches high, evidently formed of Roman earth, and containing about a pint; it is now in my possession. How this coffin came thus enclosed in the centre of a mass of chalk cliff, and at such a great distance from the surface, is matter of astonishment, and more than I can any way explain.*

In the 19th century the chalk cliff has revealed further treasures from the past, such as fragments of pottery, minor artefacts, coins and the bronze statuette of a wingless cupid. Derek Barnard, in his book *Merrily to Frendsbury* tells us that, while excavating for the canal dock in 1819, the Roman road was found that linked this villa to Watling Street at Rochester Bridge. The Romans used mortar between the stones of their buildings, and one of the main constituents of this mortar was lime, achieved by burning chalk. With a plentiful supply at Frindsbury, the first quarry was dug here by the Romans.

\* \* \* \* \*

*A singular custom used to be annually observed on May-Day by the boys of Frindsbury, and the neighbouring town of Stroud; they met on Rochester bridge, where a skirmish ensued between them.*

This custom goes back to the reign of Edward I, when a long drought caused such hardship that the monks of St Andrew's Priory agreed, amongst themselves, to make a solemn procession to Frindsbury to pray to God for rain: . . . *but the day proving windy they apprehended their lights would be blown out, their banners tossed about, and their order much discomposed.*

Due to the inclement weather, the Prior of St Andrews asked permission of the Master of the hospital at Strood to pass through their walled orchard. This hospital was founded by Glanvill, Bishop of Rochester, in 1193, and historically the priory and the hospital were often in dispute. On this occasion, the Master of Strood hospital granted the monks permission to pass through the orchard, but failed to tell his brethren. When word got out that the monks planned to 'trespass' through the hospital orchard, all the ill-feelings between the institutions came to a head and the brethren:

*. . . instantly hired a company of ribalds, armed with clubs and bats, who waylaid the poor Monks in the orchard, and gave them a severe beating. The Monks desisted from preceeding that way, but soon after found out a pious mode of revenge, by obliging the men of Frindsbury, with due humility, to come yearly on Whit-Monday, with their clubs, in procession, to Rochester, as a pennance for their crimes.*

There are other partisan versions of the story, but what started as a humiliation became a tradition, for in the 16th century, the boys of Frindsbury and Strood met every Mayday to have a faction fight, whether between themselves or against the boys of Rochester is not known.

In 1576, the historian William Lambarde wrote: 'I do not marvel if the monks sought to carry their procession through Strood again for avoiding the wind. For indeed it could not blow more boisterously out of any quarter. And thus out of this tragic history arose the byword of "Frendsbury Clubs" a term not yet forgotten.'

It is an interesting conjecture that the monks made their procession to Frindsbury on a night when the rising wind almost certainly promised a change in the weather. Their prayers for rain would, therefore, be promptly answered.

# Temple Farm, Strood

*From Temple Farm on the western banks of the Medway, the majestic ruins of Rochester castle, its venerable bridge, and cathedral, appear combined in a very advantageous point of view. The white and mouldering cliff on which the castle stands is beautifully broken by the verdant clumps of trees that here and there diversify the chalky margin of a stream, which losing its impetuosity, may be truly denominated a 'Gentle river'.*

Temple Farm today lies at the centre of a maze of 20th century brick and steel. Deep in the heart of Strood's industrial estate, approached via a netted iron gate, the ancient house of the Knights Templars sits on a suburban piece of grass between road and railway. Above the larch-lap boundary fence, a shiny board gleefully advertises The Drainage Centre, while across the road Pacific Homecare sprawls in close proximity. Strood itself is the Mecca of the D.I.Y. superstore, packed round with McDonald's, takeaway restaurants and second-hand car lots. The lush meadows leading to the banks of the *gentle river* have vanished, and the view of Rochester and the Medway in Ireland's sketch can best be appreciated by the members of Strood Yacht Club. Today, the manor looks onto an overgrown railway embankment only feet from the building. Where once meadows met the river, several working barges, converted like mini-hulks, sprout potted plants and washing, their owners enjoying a view that has changed little in 200 years.

The Dutch gables and timber-framed farm of Ireland's sketch have gone, leaving a sandwich-like building with 17th century red brick ends and a 13th century stone middle. Inside, it is easier to imagine it as the prestigious house and estate which Henry II gave to the Knights Templars in 1159. Situated so close to the Medway, and on the main road to the continent, it made a good lodge for Templars travelling on business.

The Knights Templars were an order of celibate soldiers living under a stern monastic discipline. They were established during the Crusades to protect the Holy Places and the pilgrims who visited them. In 1312, the Order of Templars was dissolved and Pope Clement V granted all their lands and goods to another religious order, the Knights Hospitallers. In the 15th century, the farmhouse was enlarged, a timber wing added and the great barn rebuilt, with farmers rather than nobles as the occupants. None of these additions are visible today.

At the end of the 18th century Ireland tells us:

*Only a small part of the mansion remains, which is converted into a farm house, where one large room, up stairs, which over-looks the river, appears to be of the time of Elizabeth, and has since that period undergone little alteration.*

*Temple Farm, Strood*

Temple Farm remained well cared for and fairly isolated in a fine garden until the early 1930s, when the City of Rochester acquired what was left of the estate for industrial development. In 1938 a committee was formed to preserve the house but their efforts were interrupted by the Second World War. During this period, neglect and hooligans caused havoc. The great barn disintegrated, the roof of the manor collapsed, and the timber wing was beyond repair. In 1951, the original stone building was restored and the external staircase added. It is now cared for by English Heritage.

Inside a dusty room at the top of the staircase, a black and white photograph shows the extent to which the building had decayed in the 1940s. The guide describes the rebuilt house as 'a respectable example of early 13th century architecture, on two floors, a high upper storey and a low vaulted undercroft'. There is, however, no communication between the undercroft and the hall above, and no internal division on either floor. It is thought that these areas were kept separate for the accommodation of a dignitary in transit, rather than for permanent habitation.

The ancient upper hall looks remarkably like a chapel with arched windows and dividing pillars. The 17th century fireplace appears stranded in the middle of the room with its brick chimney looking ill at ease among the high rafters; below, the vaulted undercroft is reminiscent of a crypt. The chill air and dusty floor gives a frisson of the secretive Templars themselves. More tangible evidence of human habitation is apparent on one wall; here boats, compasses, and a name which might be Cray are just visible. Who knows what weighty deals were signed beneath this vaulted roof, for the power of the Templars was legendary in the 13th century? Their intellectual, financial and martial prowess was such that even kings submitted to their authority. It was likely that Henry II gave Strood Manor to the Templars for, like many European sovereigns, he was in their debt. An elusive powerful elite, they were feared and respected across Europe by both Church and State. This covert Order, shrouded in myth and mystery, intrigues us as much today as it did 600 years ago.

Ireland's comments on the undercroft were brief:

*Beneath this building is a spacious vault of stone and chalk, in which the Knights Templars occasionally assembled; and, though of very ancient date, is yet in a perfect state of preservation. Its walls are of a great thickness, and the groined arches . . . have suffered little from the depridations of time.*

And on Strood itself: *In the town of Stroud little occurs worth recording . . .*

However, Ireland does comment on the oyster fishing industry, no doubt recalling the dearth of oysters for consumption in Queenborough:

*Stroud is principally supported by the oyster fishery, which is conducted by a company called Free Dredgers. Seven years apprenticeship entitles to the freedom of this company;*

*all persons catching oysters, who are not members, are subject to a penalty, and are termed cable hangers. The company frequently buy brood or spat from other parts, which they lay in this river, where they soon arrive at maturity. Holland, Westphalia, and other countries are from hence supplied with great quantities of oysters.*

*Oyster boats off Strood pier*

These rules were cited in an Act of Parliament, passed in 1728, 'for regulating, well ordering, governing, and improving the Oyster Fishery in the River Medway and waters thereof' . They were very strict, and limits were set on the quantity of oysters each dredge man should take and was known as 'setting the stint' which may have been the origin of the word "stingy". Although much has recently been done to improve the quality of the water in the Medway, Samuel Ireland would not find fresh oysters here today.

\* \* \* \* \*

In 1788, five years before Ireland's book was written, there was a proposal to connect the Thames and Medway with a canal, to protect the ships working between Chatham,

Deptford and Woolwich dockyards from attacks by the French. Ralf Dadd, the enthusiastic but unsuccessful engineer, planned a cutting through the chalk hills moving 600,000 cubic yards of spoil at a cost of £24,576. He sold the idea by stating that it would save a forty-seven mile journey and be strategically useful for carrying troops and military equipment. In 1808, another engineer, Ralf Walker, recommended that a tunnel should be dug from Higham Street into Strood Marsh to the south of Frindsbury Church.

Work on the tunnel started in April 1819 and by November 1820 the leader tunnel had been cut through the chalk. At two-and-a-half miles long, it was the largest in the country, with a towpath running the entire length. The excavated material was used to reclaim the marsh, filling in the area from St Mary's Church, Strood, to the river, and the considerable leftovers were loaded onto ships as ballast, free of charge. The basin at Frindsbury was still in use in the 1960s when ships' cargoes were unloaded directly onto railway trucks in the Strood sidings.

The canal was officially opened with much pomp and ceremony on 4 October 1824, having cost ten times the original estimate, and could take barges up to sixty tons. In his speech at the 'handsome dinner' at the Crown Inn, Rochester, Sir C. Fowler declared:

> There have been united two of the most valuable rivers in the kingdom, and two of the richest rivers in the world . . . he trusted, that the great work, besides being of use to the commerce of the country, would be of particular value to the ancient City of Rochester . . .

The canal, however, did not prosper. Tolls were too high to recover building costs, and because barges could only leave and enter at high tide, it was often quicker to sail the long way round. With the advent of the railways, the canal's fate was sealed. Notwithstanding, in 1845, the pro-active Company Proprietors of the Thames and Medway Canal renamed themselves, The Gravesend and Rochester Railway and Canal Company and built the first railway to reach the Medway towns. In 1846, the South Eastern Railway Company bought the whole enterprise for £310,000, filled in the canal and laid a double track in its place, running either ferries or coaches to connect the people of Rochester to their trains. In 1987, after twenty years of neglect, the basin was filled in. It had been large enough to take ships up to 300 tons and must have resembled a defoliated pine forest, shrouded in a web of sails, stays and rigging. The romantic Thames barges, workhorses of the Medway, shifted cargoes of cement, bricks, paper, wood, plant and equipment to fuel the growing Medway industries. In the 19th and early 20th centuries, the banks of this *gentle river* would have been as thickly forested with brick chimneys as the water was with masts, for the Lower Medway Valley was becoming the most highly industrialised part of Kent. Today, new homes and light industry spread along the banks of the Medway below the quarried chalk escarpment of Frindsbury. The sparse entrails of the old lock gates rot and rust on the grey silt, along with careening supermarket trolleys and warped barbed wire. A cemented footpath crosses the urban decay. A sad epitaph for such a great endeavour.

*Old lock gates, Strood*

On the west bank, upstream from Strood, the Medway Valley Leisure Park bears witness to the late 20th century. Above the sea lavenders and spurges of Temple Marsh, cinemas, health-and-fitness clubs, pubs and nightclubs sprout from synthetic tiles. The Centenary Walk, a paved walkway built in 1996, gives the river an urban feel. From the balcony of the pub there is an uninterrupted view across the broad stretch of water to the Medway Marina where slit-eyed, pointed-nose pleasure craft rock lightly on the water. Sitting heavily on the grey mud, a few geriatric barges, in various stages of decay, await death or resurrection.

Through the wide arches of the soaring Medway Bridge, there remains a stretch of Ireland's Medway. Chatham, Rochester, Strood and Borstal have been left downstream, leaving only Wouldham Marshes, gently rising hills, lapwings and a few fishermen. On the west bank, Cuxton does not yet intrude and the tall chimney of a cement works merely accentuates the wide sweep of the river. An electric train slows into Cuxton's unmanned and sleepy station, and the barriers swing across the small road to let it pass. Cuxton Marina surrounds an old paper-mill along the path, a reminder of the Medway's indigenous industry. In Ireland's time, the demand for paper was rising as the wool industry declined. The same water-mills that had agitated wool and fuller's earth were adapted to pulp linen rags for making paper. In 1800, there were about twenty paper-mills in the Maidstone area, most of which used the Medway for transporting their goods.

The few boats which have survived from the days when the Medway was a transport system have had to change with the times. One example is the *Rochester Queen,* originally named *M.V. Coronia,* and subsequently *Bournemouth Queen* and *Queen of Scots* showing that she has played many parts in her fifty-three years. In the Second World War she saw service, both as a boom defence vessel, and a detention ship for recalcitrant sailors, and in peacetime has been an escort for the Royal Yacht *Britannia.* At the present time she is enjoying a new lease of life as a floating restaurant and pub at Cuxton.

From the steaming, belching paper factory at Snodland, the Medway shrinks between marshy strips of land, mud and reed banks. Here the river loops in a great meander called Horseshoe Reach. On the east bank, there is an uncluttered view of the chalk escarpments of Burham Down and Bluebell Hill, little-changed since the pilgrims walked along the Downs to Rochester and Canterbury, and Horsa was buried at Kit's Coty. Only the ubiquitous pylons, and great bundles of newspapers, scattered across the landscape, suggest the 20th century. Ireland's description of Burham is very similar: . . . *Passing Snodeland, the lowly situation of Burham church, produces a beautiful effect; the high chalk and gravelly bank, which form the margin of the river, give a good foreground to the landscape; while, in the distance, a fine screen of hills running nearly parallel with the river terminates the scene.*

*Signal box at Snodland station*

Between Snodland and Aylesford, the Medway disappears amongst brackish tidal vegetation and muddy banks. At low tide, the imposing river, which flows so confidently through Rochester, narrows to a mere stream much as it did in Ireland's day . . . *At New Hythe the river scenery conveys to the mind more the idea of a stream running through a garden, than that of a navigable river.*

Snodland itself is one of the industrial blots on the Medway landscape. However, All Saints' Church, with its 14th century tower rising by the river, remains a gentle rebuke to the cement and paper industries which engulf it. Ferry Cottage marks the spot where pilgrims once crossed the river on their way to Rochester and Canterbury. The weather-boarded cottage, its tiny garden bright with hollyhocks, looks over the reed-filled river to the rising ground of the unspoiled east bank. Back in prehistoric times, it is possible that there was once a ford here for travellers to cross the Medway along what is called the Pilgrim's Way. Now walkers on this ancient path keep their feet dry, high above the river, as they share the cantilevered Medway Bridge with a stream of motorway traffic.

*Ferry Cottage, Snodland*

# Lord Darnley's Mausoleum at Cobham Park

*This expensive stone edifice is from a design of the ingenious Mr. Wyatt, and is in the Doric order; its parts and ornaments are judiciously placed, and cannot fail to attract the attention as well as command the admiration of every observer of taste.*

This extraordinary *edifice* was built between 1783 and 1789, only a few years before Ireland made his sketch. The story goes that on his deathbed in 1781, the 3rd Earl of Darnley asked his son to build a mausoleum to keep all the family together in death.

The best way to approach this morbid extravaganza is on foot from Cobham village, up the rutted path of William's Hill, and then through a wood of old oaks and chestnut trees. Suddenly, the silence is obliterated by the roar of motorbikes, revving and bumping over the rough ground; a stream of leather-clad youngsters appears on their noisy chargers, grinning as their machines buck and sway. Slowly, the 20th century roar dies into the thickening woods and, deep in the trees, a clearing on the hilltop reveals a surreal Egyptian-style mausoleum with Doric pillars and pyramidal roof; a mirage on the hilltop.

No doubt the woods in the 18th century were less dense, and the mausoleum would not have been stumbled upon as if the visitor was transported to C.S. Lewis's *Land of Narnia*. While admiring this lavish mausoleum, Ireland dismissed the pyramidal top as *ponderous and unmeaning; and . . . would have had a more pleasing, and certainly more classical effect, had it been finished with a circular dome: I am informed this angular top is to be removed*, he adds hopefully. Determined to impress his readers, he continues:

*The upper part of this building is intended as a family chapel; . . . beneath it is the burial vault, in which are recesses intended to receive the last remains of human greatness; . . . a scene where (if such a wish had ever existed, but in the flight of poetry) 'kings for such a tomb would wish to die'.*

Both Lord Darnley and Samuel Ireland would have been horrified to see the 'dying tomb' today. As the visitor approaches, the magic evaporates. The pot-holed path around the building is now a circuit for motor and mountain-bikes; youths, struggling to keep their balance, yell obscenities which match the explicit graffiti on the smooth, white walls of the mausoleum. The coat of arms has gone, the fabric is crumbling, and the cavernous burial vault, like some prolapsed intestine, is filled only with fallen bricks, dogs' dirt and litter. The empty recesses, for the *last remains of human greatness,* yawn darkly in the cold, damp air, waiting to turn to dust and decay. Despite the grand design, this mausoleum was never consecrated or used and, in 1985, the present Lord Darnley sold it to a developer for residential conversion. Following the developer's bankruptcy, the *expensive stone edifice* is now in the hands of a receiver, its future in the balance.

The ever-practical Ireland tells us: *This celebrated mausoleum is reported to have cost ten thousand pounds.* In fact the 4th Earl who commissioned the mausoleum, spent £30,000 on this white elephant. After its completion, the Bishop of Rochester, disapproving of burials in secular settings, refused to consecrate a building that so brazenly evoked pagan arcady. As a result, the platform, constructed in a deep basement for Lord Darnley's coffin, has never been occupied.

Emerging from the woods, the walker looks over the *noble park of Cobham spread below.* The scene appears timeless, yet the busy A2 Dartford to Rochester trunk-road, originally the old Roman road of Watling Street and later the turnpike road, passes the main entrance to Cobham Hall and Park. The mellow bricks, tall chimneys and four, domed towers of the Elizabethan Hall rise from the cedars and oaks of an elegant park. Woods, rolling hills, and the great mansion make a stage-set where galloping Tudor huntsmen would not seem out of place. Although now a girls' boarding-school, Cobham Hall has lost none of its grandeur. Sir John de Cobham, Sir John Oldcastle, Sir Walter Raleigh and later, Charles Dickens, have all enjoyed the beauty of this park. In its heyday it covered an area of 18,000 acres and in 1698 the timber alone was valued at £5,000.

Mr Ireland then turns his attention to the *noble family mansion* whose name derives from its former possessors, *the eminent family of Cobham, who, from historical accounts as early as King John, have in every department filled the highest posts of trust and honour with superior lustre to themselves, and credit to their country.*

In the reign of James I, Henry Brooke, Lord Cobham together with his brother George, Sir Walter Raleigh and others were accused of conspiring to kill the king, brought to trial at Winchester and condemned to death. George was beheaded, but

Lord Cobham was sentenced to life imprisonment in the Tower of London where he died in 1619, forfeiting his estates to the Crown.

*The manor, with Cobham Hall, came thus by attainder to the Crown, from whence it was granted to Lodowick Stuart, Duke of Lenox, kinsman to James I, from whose family, by intermarriages, it devolved to its present noble possessor, the Earl of Darnley.*

These Darnleys were of Irish descent, and the title was created for them in 1725.

*Cobham Hall*

An old legend, from the days when the Knights Templars flourished in the 12th century, links Cobham Hall with Temple Manor at Strood. Sir Reginald Braybrooke, a member of the Knights Templars, was riding from Cobham Hall to Temple Manor at Strood by a lonely path, when an arrow pierced his heart, mortally wounding him. His assassin was never discovered, in spite of strenuous efforts by his fellow Templars. Years later, on a bitterly cold night, a priest, who was one of the brethren of Templars, sought shelter at a poor hovel in Luddesdown village. The old woman who lived there was herself sick and dying, and the Templar noticed that the rich coverlet over her bed was the cloak of Sir Reginald himself. She confessed that her husband had been his assassin, committing the deed from some fancied wrong. However, from that day on, his conscience gave him no peace and a few months later his body was found at the bottom of a nearby chalk-pit. When the old woman died, the priest took Sir Reginald's cloak to the temple, where it was long preserved by the knights as a relic of their martyred brother.

Near the mausoleum was once the site of an unusual epitaph to the 5th Earl of Darnley known as the Toe Monument. It was here, in 1835, that the unfortunate young earl stopped to show some companions how to use an axe properly, and succeeded in chopping off two of his own toes. He contracted tetanus, and died four days later at the age of thirty-nine.

A more recent anecdote comes from the world of cricket. The much-prized Ashes were the private property of the Hon. Ivo Bligh, who became the 8th Earl of Darnley. The Ashes date from 1882; when England, as yet unbeaten on her own soil, played a test-match against Australia and lost. The following day a mock obituary in the Sporting Times announced that English Cricket had died at the Oval on 29 August 1882; Ivo Bligh set off for Australia a few weeks later to recover the mythical Ashes. The three return matches were played over Christmas and New Year 1882-3. England duly won the series, and a group of ladies from Melbourne burnt one of the bails used in the victorious third match. As a joke, these were placed in a small brown pottery urn and presented to Ivo Bligh, who solemnly placed them on his study mantelpiece at Cobham Hall. His successor was not interested in cricket, and the urn that contained them was relegated to the storeroom until it was presented to the museum at Lord's Cricket Ground in 1927 when Ivo died. Rumour has it that, during their sojourn at the Hall, the precious Ashes were spilt when a servant was dusting the mantelpiece, and later topped up by a perspicacious butler from one of his Lordship's fireplaces.

A romantic sequel to the 1882-3 tour occurred on the 9 February 1884, when the Hon. Ivo Bligh married Miss Florence Rose Morphy, one of the ladies who burnt the bail and so inaugurated the famous Ashes.

Cobham Hall itself impressed Samuel Ireland greatly.

*The centre of this stately building is the work of Inigo Jones; the staircase is spacious, and the music gallery is richly adorned with ornaments well conceived for grandeur of effect . . . the wings are of more ancient date, but have been new cased with brick, and rendered uniform with the other part of the building.*

However, it may be that his facts were not entirely correct, for the centre of the building was not by Inigo Jones, but by his pupil John Webb circa 1670. Further additions to the central storey were added in 1770 by Sir W. Chambers. Later, James Wyatt added two extra wings creating an H-shape, and then a further stable-block to link the eastern ends, so creating a courtyard and retaining the symmetry of the building. In the early 19th century, Wyatt and the Reptons carried out alterations to make the building look much older, including forging some of the date stones.

*Cobham Hall, with the outhouses, is reported to have cost sixty thousand pounds. The park is large, but not so extensive as formerly; it is famed for its stately timber trees, particularly its oaks, some of which are upwards of twenty feet in circumference; and by their venerable appearance justify the poet's opinion:*

'The monarch oak,
Three centuries he grows, and three he stays
Supreme in state, and in three more decays.'

A few ancient oaks survive, dating from about 1550, but there would have been many more 200 years ago. There was, in Ireland's time, a remarkable chestnut tree in the Park known as the Four Sisters, so called because of its four large arms or trunks. It was thirty-two feet (9·754 metres) in circumference, but sadly, this great specimen fell down in 1884. More recently, the great storm in the autumn of 1987 felled most of the last of the five avenues of limes, originally planted by the 6th Duke of Lennox in 1660 when he developed the park and rebuilt the centre of the house. Fortunately, the trees were rapidly replanted, ensuring the survival of the avenue. At the end of the 18th century, the 4th Earl employed the celebrated landscape gardener, Humphrey Repton, to restore the park to its present naturalised state. The beautiful Cedar of Lebanon, standing before the west front of the house, is 190 years old.

Perhaps feeling hungry, Ireland mentions the deer . . . *the venison of this park is, from the quality of the herbage on which it is fed, esteemed to be superior in flavour to that of almost any other in the country*. Longhorn cattle and a herd of 800 fallow deer once enjoyed 830 acres of parkland. Their graceful forms were an integral part of the landscape from the 13th century, when Cobham was a Norman manor house. The great park, once stretching from the Thames to the Medway, has now shrunk to a mere 150 acres, and daffodils replace the deer which were consumed during the Second World War.

This century has seen a decline in the fortunes of Cobham Hall. In the First World War it was used as a hospital, and during the Second World War as a billet for Battle of Britain pilots. In 1955, it was handed over to the Government in lieu of death duties on the death of the 9th Earl. The contents were sold by Sothebys in 1957, when the Ministry of Public Works and Buildings took it over to repair and restore some of the structure. The property was then leased to the Westward Educational Trust, and later sold to them for use as an independent school for girls. The upkeep of this house and park is costly; in 1983 The Cobham Hall Heritage Trust was set up enabling much-needed clearing and replanting to be undertaken in the park. The Hall is used for income-generating activities outside school terms such as craft fairs, weddings, guided tours, and music making.

Today, the great Elizabethan house grapples with the 20th century; computers, stacking chairs and school bags range beside the magnificent marble fireplaces, built by a Flemish craftsman Giles de Witt at the end of the 16th century. The door into the 133 feet long (40·5 metres) library, is lined with fake leather-bound books, and the state dressing-room still has 1790 Chinese wallpaper and a gold brocade four-poster bed. The cracked Adams-style ceiling of the state bedchamber, where Charles I and his wife Maria, spent the first night of their honeymoon, looks down on temporary partitions festooned with art work. The panelled dining room has marble alcoves, where coyly draped statues stare down upon the young diners. The jewel in the crown is the Gilt Hall, where wall-to-wall marble drips with gold swags, and a wealth of Corinthian columns stand like ' wallflowers' below a richly-decorated gilt ceiling. It is the perfect place for chamber music, where the 20th century casual dress is the only jarring note. Above the fireplace, two elegant young men look down on the audience. They are the ill-fated Stuart boys, Lords Bernard and John, sons of Esme 3rd Duke of Lennox and his wife Katherine. They both died during the Civil War. This copy of the original Van Dyke portrait perhaps typifies this handsome but sad house whose owners have not lived happily ever after. The conspirator, Henry Brooke, who died in 1619, had the prophetic words: 'EACH MAN MAKES FOR HIMSELF HIS OWN SHIPWRECK', carved into one of de Witt fireplaces, and these words can still be seen today. The four great families of Cobham Hall, the de Cobhams, the Brookes of Cobham, the Dukes of Lennox and the Darnleys have been through some stormy seas, and a pall of sadness hangs over the mellow bricks of their treasured home.

Ireland omits to mention the old village of Cobham and deals with the church in one sentence: *In Cobham Church are several well sculptured monuments of the Cobham family, some of them in a superior style of execution..*

This hardly does justice to the church which was rebuilt from money provided by the de Cobhams. It was restored in the 14th century by Sir John de Cobham and is full of surprises. The spacious chancel dates from 1220 and is bordered with a unique collection of brasses, some of which are more than 600 years old. Sir John certainly deserves to be remembered, for he also founded the college for priests behind the church, built Cooling Castle and helped to build Rochester Bridge.

Apart from the size of the chancel, the magnificent Elizabethan table-tomb in the centre of the great space would do credit to royalty. Lying in state on this alabaster and black marble are the supine figures of George Brooke, Lord Cobham and his wife, Anne Bray, their hands folded neatly in prayer, their feet resting daintily on an antelope and a lion. Between the black pillars down the sides of the tomb kneel the couple's ten children. The first is William, 10th Lord Cobham, founder of the Alms-houses (the New College) and Cobham Hall. His grandson, William Brooke, was disinherited by James I and fought on the Parliament side in the Civil War, which

Plate IX

Leybourne Castle

Plate X

Malling Abbey

Plate XI

Aylesford

Plate XII

Maidstone

Plate XIII

Boxley Abbey

Plate XIV

Leeds Castle

Plate XV

East Farleigh

Plate XVI

Teston

may explain why these brasses have survived. In the 18th century, a traveller records that they were bundled up in an ancient chest, and Hasted, the Kent historian quoted so much by Ireland, found that workmen mending the roof were also purloining the brasses. They were not on show in Ireland's time, for the collection we see today was re-laid in the 1860s at the expense of Mr F.C. Brooke, a descendant of the medieval family.

Behind the church, the grey stones of an ancient building blend into the uncut grass and nettles. A low arch leads the explorer to a surprisingly neat quadrangle where the mullioned windows of twenty-one identical one-up-one-down houses stare at each other across a neat square of grass. Each identical wooden door, set in a low stone arch, is named after local villages like Hoo, Cliffe and Cobham, and a row of bright bedding-plants dress the stone footings like the icing round the border of a cake. These are the alms-houses, converted from the old college, built by the industrious Sir John de Cobham in 1362. The present alterations were completed in 1598. A lopsided tiled porch at the front of the building leads through a massive oak door to the old hall, where trestle-tables and chairs wait expectantly in front of the ancient stone fireplace. Electric light bulbs sprout incongruously from the circular iron ceiling light and a life-size portrait gazes down from the high, white wall onto the emptiness of this strange room which, in 1598, was retained as a meeting-place for the pensioners of the 'New College'. This tradition has continued for, in 1992, a site was purchased in the adjoining Stonehouse Yard, and sixteen new flats were built and opened by the Bishop of Rochester in 1994.

Now the church bells ring out across the tombstones and down the old village street where Dickens read from his novel, *Pickwick Papers,* at The Leather Bottle pub. It was to this pub that the lovelorn Mr Tupman fled after being jilted by Rachel Wardle, and drowned his sorrows in Mr Pickwick's company.

The oldest pub in the village is the Darnley Arms. Built in 1196, it served as a hostelry until the demise of coaches early in the 20th century. The resident ghost is reputed to be the 15th century knight, Sir Thomas Kemp, (1410-1470), a relation of the sovereign. Sentenced to death, he spent his last night at the inn, en route for Rochester where he was to have been executed. Given a last minute reprieve, he returned to live out his days at the Darnley Arms and appears to have been reluctant to leave.

The religious persecutions of the 16th and 17th centuries led to many tunnels being dug in the area, intended as 'bolt-holes' for the persecuted. One such tunnel is known to have run between the old college, behind the church, and thence to the Darnley Arms cellar. As Cobham Church was never sacked, it is rumoured that the tunnel was used by the college monks as a 'bolt-hole' for storing secret tipple.

Folded into an unspoiled corner of history, Gravesham district villages like Cobham and Luddesdown, have miraculously escaped the 20th century.

# The Remains of Halling House

*Passing the ancient village of Woldham, . . . little variation of scenery occurs, till we approach the extensive ruins of Halling-house, formerly one of the four splendid residences of the Bishops of Rochester . . . the remains of which are only to be traced by fragments of ruinated walls.*

The Romans settled along this fertile stretch and grew vines. Their villas have been discovered in the area, and it seems that the Medway was a flourishing commercial waterway in Roman times. Our self-educated artist informs us that, in the 14th century, Hamo de Heth, then Bishop of Rochester, extended the *splendid residence* by adding a hall and chapel . . . *This simple edifice and these humble roofs, dedicated only to God and Religion, yet remain. The loftier domes and marble towers, in which hierarchy, the invention of man, lifted its mitred form, having mouldered away.*

Hamo, it seems, was something of a bon viveur. According to Ireland, he was confessor to King Edward II . . . *in the nineteenth year of his reign . . . our sumptous Bishop . . . sent him thither a present of his drinks, and withal both wine and grapes of his own growth from his vineyard at Halling.*

From this, Ireland surmises that the word *Vinae*, (mentioned in the Domesday Book) meant something more than a mere plantation of apples and pears . . . *and, it may be reasonably supposed that from its contiguity to France, the attempt to naturalise this seducing and delicious stranger, would first be made in this county . . .*

Halling, (pronounced Hauling) we are told, derived its name from its healthy situation and signifies a wholesome, low place or meadow. William Lambarde, the 16th century historian, lived for some time in Halling House and Ireland quotes him as saying: *At this place of the Bishop in Halling, I am drawing on the last scene of my life, where God hath given me liberorum quadrigam, all the fruite that ever I had.*

It was in this region of the Medway that Ireland has appositely quoted from Sir Richard Blackmore's poem about the river:

'Whose wanton tide in wreathing volumes flows,
Still forming reedy islands as it goes.
And in meanders to the neighbouring plain,
The liquid serpent draws its silver train.'

*The Church of St John the Baptist, Halling*

The meandering *liquid serpent* no longer *draws its silver train* through fields of hops, and orchards. Houses are rising from the fields, and pylons replace the hop poles. There are no vines here, although there are vineyards farther upstream near Penshurst and Lamberhurst. Today, it is not only bishops who enjoy the *seducing and delicious stranger*. Beer and wine are imported from all over the world and consumed in vast quantities by a large percentage of the population. It is easy for all those who live in Kent to cross the Channel on ferries or through the tunnel, and fill their cars with duty-free liquor. A less seducing stranger in 1997 was the proposed waste-to-energy incinerator that Kent County Council planned to install at Halling. Their application was turned down, and a quarry near Allington is now a proposed site for this sophisticated method of recycling.

Two hundred years on, all trace of Halling House has now *mouldered away*. Arthur Mee in his *King's England* series on Kent says of Halling: 'An unlovely place, which has put its name in history, perhaps the only bit of beauty here is just through the lych-gate, where the church stands on a mound, huddled round with tasteless bricks and mortar.'

The only visible remains of the old palace is a stone wall bounding the neat churchyard, though no doubt there is more rubble beneath the nettles in the few trees behind the church. With Ireland's sketch and a lot of imagination, it is possible to visualise a scene that was, as Mee puts it, '. . . as fair as any in Kent'.

*Rugby Cement works at Halling*

# Malling Abbey

*The venerable remains of this abbey, in the annexed sketch, are taken in so different a point of view from all others that have come to my knowledge, that I flatter myself it will, in its place, be as acceptable as any yet presented to the public.*

Malling Abbey, built in 1090, was the earliest religious house in the Maidstone area. Like Rochester Cathedral, it was built by Gundulf, Bishop of Rochester. The land which he chose for his Benedictine foundation at Malling had been given to the Diocese of Rochester by Edmund, King of Mercia, in 945. An anecdote from Ireland about the original charter of the lands of this manor is worth quoting:

*This charter, after having been signed by the King, the Archbishops, and Bishops, is then signed by AEfgifu, the King's concubine, who there describes herself 'Ego AElfgifu concubina Regis affui'.*

Concubinage, far from being a disgrace was, it seems, accepted in those days. A custom Ireland feels must have come from the laws of the Romans, who were not allowed to marry a woman *greatly inferior in birth and condition, yet permitted to keep her as a concubine.*

Here, Ireland again voices his prejudices:

*Popes have allowed concubines: and the Council of Toledo have humanely given a man permission to keep one woman without excommunication, in case she should serve him as a wife. This relaxation of the austerity in religious manners, inclines one to think, that, in announcing their indulgencies, these holy fathers and synods were not unmindful of themselves . . .*

Surrogate mothers are nothing new it seems, though in those days they were not paid for their labours.

Later, Bishop Gundulf gave the land to the nuns of St Mary's Abbey, but did not appoint an abbess until he was on his deathbed. Ireland continues with a story which evidently surprised him, even in the 18th century:

*Bishop Gundolph was unwilling to trust a female to preside over this abbey during his life, continued himself as governor, and, when nearly at the point of death, empowered one Avicia to take upon herself the character of Abbess after his decease; but even to her he refused delivering either the pastoral staff, gloves or ring, till she had promised canonical obedience to the See of Rochester, and had taken an oath not to admit either Abbess or Nun into the house without the consent and privity of his successor.*

Records of the abbey's first four centuries are slight. Gundulf's successors, it appears, intervened regarding the over-generous admission of corrodians, (persons who paid to live in the abbey precincts as permanent guests). These guests helped the abbey's finances, but were not always suited to life in a religious house. The Bishop of Rochester restricted the grant of corrodies, and kept a watchful eye on the Abbess.

What Ireland omits to tell us is that a disastrous fire in West Malling in 1190 destroyed much of the town and seriously damaged many of the abbey buildings. Later, the first cases of the Black Death occurred in Kent in 1348 and the terrible disease decimated the nuns of Malling Abbey, reducing the community to four professed nuns and four novices. It seems miraculous that the community survived until 1538, when Henry VIII's commissioners forced the abbey to surrender to the Crown.

The property then passed into secular hands. By the end of the 17th century the magnificent church had almost disappeared, and the great tower at the west end fell into ruin. In the 18th century, the abbey belonged to the Honeywood family, and Ireland tells us that:

*Mr Frazer Honeywood, banker of London, has, within a few years, almost rebuilt the abbeyhouse as a family residence in the gothic style, leaving many of the ancient buildings and offices standing; part of the house appears in the annexed view.*

Today, Frazer Honeywood's *family residence*, which incorporates the arcades of the 13th century cloister, is part of the enclosure of the Anglican Benedictine nuns who live and work there. The 14th century pilgrim chapel beside the gatehouse has been used at different times as a meeting-house and a joiner's workshop. It was restored in 1858 by the Akers family.

In 1892, the abbey was purchased by Miss Charlotte Boyd, a wealthy and devout woman of vision and, by her gift, Malling Abbey once again became a religious house for Benedictine nuns.

The nuns still continue their tradition of hospitality. Visitors are warmly received, and every year about 2,000 people come to the guest house for spiritual renewal. Entering the well-tended abbey grounds is a memorable experience. Through the arch of the 14th century gatehouse, the great tower built by Bishop Gundulf 900 years ago is a breathtaking remnant of history. The warm Kentish ragstone, mellow and crumbling, shows off the turrets, niches and arcading which echo Gundulf's design for the west front of Rochester Cathedral. Miraculously, this great remnant has been stitched back into a living, worshipping community of Benedictine nuns. Thus, nine centuries after Bishop Gundulf established it as one of the first such communities for women founded after the Norman Conquest, it remains an unchanged microcosm of God's creation.

At the end of the 20th century, some thirty nuns from home and abroad, live out the values of the Gospel and the 6th century Rule of St Benedict. They tend the fertile grounds, bake bread, grow vegetables, pray and worship. Their present abbey church, built in 1966, is a combination of simplicity and austerity. The light interior provides a holy space where the nuns renew their faith seven times a day. Their unaccompanied plainsong chants give a sense of continuity and stability in this peaceful place, where prayer has been valid for so many centuries.

Neatly banked with spring flowers, the waters of the Ewell flow through the abbey grounds, leaving the boundary wall of the estate down an impressive cascade, built in 1810. Once back in the secular world, the water pours into an unimpressive ditch beside the busy road. Inside the ancient walls, there is a feeling of 'apartness': of peace and God-centred quiet, where only birdsong and running water are heard in the orchards and walled gardens.

The town of West Malling has changed little except for the motorcar. The wide High Street, with many 18th century houses, would be easily recognised by Samuel Ireland. Unnoticed, the ancient abbey ruins rise mysteriously behind the branches of great trees, separated from the town by a high boundary wall. In its 900 years of history, St Mary's Abbey has survived fire, plague, dissolution and decay, thanks to the hidden faith of generations of this small community of Anglican Benedictine nuns.

*The Cascade, Malling Abbey*

# Leybourne Castle

*The remains of Leyborne Castle, in this vicinage, though now merely a farm-house, and greatly in decay, is yet an object worthy of the pencil; and, even from its present appearance, painfully recalls to the mind its wasted honours and lost importance.*

Even in Ireland's time, only the stonework of the gatehouse and fragments of arches and walls, could be seen. Today, few would know of its existence. The remains of the castle, hiding behind the church, have now been sympathetically integrated into a Cotswold-style manor house, built in 1926. Although visible from the road, the castle is seldom noticed by passing motorists. A bypass is currently planned for the village which will leave this small oasis of history in peace.

The name, Leybourne, originates from the brook running beside the church and castle, Lilleburna or Lylle's stream. When Odo, Bishop of Bayeux, half-brother to William the Conqueror, was disgraced and sent home, Leybourne came into the hands of the Crown. In Richard I's reign it belonged to a famous crusader, Sir Roger de Leybourne, who built the castle. Sir Roger was a gallant knight, who defended Rochester Castle for the King against Gilbert de Tonbridge and Simon de Montfort. He died in 1271 on a crusade in Palestine, and his embalmed heart still rests in a stone casket in Leybourne Church. His son, William de Leybourne, was a friend of Edward I, and the King frequently visited him at Leybourne Castle. In 1286, Edward I made William the first English admiral. Sadly there were no heirs, although not for want of trying. In Edward III's reign, Juliana de Leybourne married no fewer than three wealthy barons. She was so rich that she earned the title of Infanta of Kent. She died possessing twelve Kentish manors but no children. The castle was then given to the Cistercian Abbey of Grace of the Blessed Virgin on Tower Hill until seized by Henry VIII at the dissolution of the monasteries . . . *from whence it has, after many changes, come into the possession of its present owner, Henry Hawley, Esq of the Grange in this parish.*

The Hawleys were vicars of Leybourne Church. Sir Joseph Hawley trained horses so successfully that they won the Derby no less than four times in the mid-18th century. The Grange became a mental hospital in the 19th century and now is the possible site for 700 residential homes. Horses from a nearby livery stable still graze the fields in a rural landscape which stretches to the rising slopes of Wrotham Hill.

The long drive sweeps round the back of the church, taking the visitor through the arch between the ragstone shells of the ancient gatehouse into a strange courtyard. The mellow stone of the 1930s house grows out of the ruin, while the empty shell of the north roundel makes an unusual garden wall. Inside the substantial house, the rooms facing the roundel are bowed inwards to complete the circle. A solitary, high building, reminiscent of a chapel, stands alone in the courtyard, possibly once the pantry and buttery of the original castle. By the back door, a fragmented chunk of ragged wall stands like a broken tooth, a reminder of the castle's heyday. Currently the house is being lovingly restored to its 1930s glory in a modern crusade to keep our heritage from decay.

# Hop Gathering

*Loa! On auxilliary poles, the hops*
*Ascending spiral, ranged in meet array!*
*Transporting prospect! These, as modern use*
*Ordains, infused, and auburn drink compose,*
*Wholesome, of deathless fame.*

Ireland, continuing up the Medway, passes Mill-Hall, near Aylesford, where his eye is *gratified with a view of the richest produce of this fruitful country, the flowery HOP.* The beauty of this plant inspired him to make his sketch of hops and hop-pickers. He waxes lyrical as he describes the scene:

*The cheerful countenance of the hop-gatherer, just quitting his labour, the younger dancing round the loaded poles; and the more aged spreading his humble repast on the scattered leaves, while each in turn,*

*Crowns high the goblet, and with cheerful draught*
*Enjoys the present hour, adjourns the future thought.*

The reader wonders how much picking went on after the *cheerful draught*.

The hop plant *was once the favourite beverage of our countrymen,* Ireland tells us, and seems to have had a somewhat chequered career since its introduction into England by the Walloons in Henry VIII's reign. At that time it was regarded as unfit for human consumption and considered 'an unwholesome weed'. Prejudices ran so high that Parliament was petitioned against 'that wicked weed called hops'. In 1524, a decree was published forbidding the use of hops in bittering beer because they tended to 'make people melancholy'. However, sanity prevailed, and the enjoyable effects of this 'auburn drink' enabled hop-farming to flourish in the first half of the 17th century. According to Hasted, their cultivation became the 'great part of the wealth of Maidstone.'

In Ireland's time, so many Flemish hops were smuggled into Kent that Maidstone hop-planters asked Parliament to pass an act preventing the importation of foreign hops. Ironically, today, Parliament sanctions an open market policy enabling hops to be imported from any part of the world. In spite of a 'Real Ale' revival, more imported lager than beer is consumed today. Cheap day-trips to French Channel ports on the Shuttle or ferry enable the inhabitants of Kent to purchase lager at a fraction of the price they pay here and bring home the booty without paying excise duty. All this means that many small hop-growers have been edged out of the market and the overall numbers have shrunk tenfold.

The cost of raising an acre of hops has always been high. Today, it is around £1,500 while in 1790 it was £20, inclusive of rents and taxes. Two hundred years ago the hop industry was booming, for in 1787, a grower from East Farleigh, who farmed forty acres at a rent of £40, sold his hops at £10 per hundredweight, realising an incredible £4,873, a huge sum in those days.

Kent remains synonymous with hops and oast-houses. At the close of the 20th century the mood is nostalgic; although fewer hops are grown, swags of the delicate lime-green hop-cones are dried and used to decorate oast-houses, preserved as homes for the wealthy. In the late 1990s the survival of the hop industry is under threat. A few derelict brick huts with peeling wallpaper, are all that remain of the hordes of migrant hoppers, mainly East-Enders, who used to spend two weeks every September, 'hopping dahn in Kent'. By the middle of the 20th century, machines were taking over from hand-pickers, and the days of the East-Enders' working holidays were numbered. Today, fewer and fewer farmers are willing to take the financial risk of growing hops, because of the fierce competition from abroad, and the increasing popularity of lager. Soon the familiar poles, with their encircling green leaves and pungent fruit, will vanish from Kentish fields, and hops will enter the domain of heritage.

Beltring Farm, Paddock Wood, was sold to Whitbread's Brewery for £8,000 in 1920 and visitors encouraged. The shire horses that delivered beer to customers in the London area were retired to Beltring, and became a further tourist attraction. In 1997, Beltring Hop Farm was sold to a private owner for £2,000,000 and has become The Hop Farm Country Park. Described as a 'proud monument to the hopping industry' it offers a Hop Story Exhibition, Gardeners' Oast and Pottery Workshop, Corporate Entertaining and Beer Festivals. The shire horses now pull brides and grooms, and hot-air ballooning gives a birds-eye view of the fifteen oast-houses with their tiled witches' hats, topped with white cowls.

It is good to know that a few breweries have survived the vicissitudes of the Kentish hop. The family-run Larkins Brewery, now operating from the owner's farm at Chiddingstone, has been growing hops since Tudor times. Currently, they supply a large number of free houses which still slake the thirst of "Men of Kent" and "Kentish Men".

# The Friars & Aylesford

This seat of the Countess of Aylesford called the Friars, described by Ireland as: *a venerable mansion which is close to the banks of the Medway, comprizing, in one point of view, the most perfect landscape I have met with on this river.*

He dedicates his book to *The Right Honorable the Countess Dowager of Aylesford* and the letter quoted below shows how much Samuel Ireland appreciated her patronage.

*MADAM,*

*As a testimony of that deference which I owe to a Patroness of the Fine Arts, and the respect and veneration due to that more exalted character of the Friend to Humanity; permit me to inscribe to your Ladyship this attempt to delineate the Picturesque Scenery of the River Medway; a river, which, though it spreads abundant fertility around the valleys through which it flows, is yet rivalled by those blessings so liberally dispensed by your beneficent hand. I am,*

*MADAM,*

*With all due Respect,*

*Your Ladyship's,*

*Very obliged and*

*Obedient Servant,*

*SAM, IRELAND.*

Without Mr Ireland's sycophancy, there may have been no *Picturesque Views on the River Medway and Works of Art in its Vicinity.*

The village of Aylesford itself claims to be England's oldest continuously occupied village. The site was chosen in neolithic times because the river was easily fordable at low tide and this feature attracted the Romans.

Ireland tells us that Aylesford Priory, or The Friars as it came to be called, was founded in Henry III's reign under the patronage of Richard, Lord Grey of Cudnor. Lord Grey visited Mount Carmel while in Palestine during the crusades and, liking the austere mode of living among the hermits there, established a similar rigid plan in Aylesford Wood. This was the first order of Friars' Carmelites in this country.

At the dissolution of the monasteries, this Priory of White Friars at Aylesford, was given to Sir Thomas Wyatt. In 1554, his son masterminded the Wyatt Rebellion against Queen Mary, and forfeited his property to the Crown as well as his head. Queen Elizabeth I gave the Priory to Mr Sidley, who gave the town its bridge, *which he built in 1607 together with an hospital. After various alienations this Priory came, at length, into the family of its present noble possessor, whose open hand has, in the feelings of the industrious poor, as much exceeded the dole indiscriminately distributed at the gates of the Priory, as her gentle virtues are in the eye of heaven more acceptable than the pious austerities of its former inhabitants.*

Flattery was as useful a tool 200 hundred years ago as it is today. After this obsequious prose, Ireland's text descends into bathos:

*Some parts of the Priory still remain, and these are most conspicuous in the kitchen and out-offices. In the church were interred many of the family of Lord Grey, of Codnor, and the Colepeppers, Etc., the monuments of the latter being well preserved.*

Ireland's sketch of the church and bridge looks upstream from the friary end. From here he tells us, *the village is happily revealed from behind a verdant intervening slope, and the gothic bridge beneath is, in part, so happily concealed by the hand of nature, as to appear the design of art.*

In 1998, the view is little changed although, in 1997, a new bridge was built close to the village to relieve the traffic flow over Ireland's *gothic bridge*. The modern version spans the river like a fallen R.S.J., contrasting with the mellow ragstone and graceful arches of its predecessor. The steeply pitched roofs of tile-clad houses cluster timelessly beneath Aylesford Church, their cottage gardens overflowing onto the towpath. The central arch of the 14th century ragstone bridge was enlarged in 1824 to ease the passage of boats heading to Maidstone. In spite of the roar from the M2 motorway and the industrial development seeping along the river banks, the old bridge and village are still a nugget of history.

Her Ladyship's seat is now a well-restored Carmelite Friary which radiates carefully nurtured peace and tranquillity. From the drive, the eye of tourist or contemporary pilgrim sweeps past the solid stone walls of shrine and chapels, ancient gatehouse, refurbished barn, to a panorama that, in Ireland's day, revealed the Medway's sweet water and fertile green pastures. Here the admirer's gaze is shattered by a mighty slab of steel covering several acres of *verdant* valley, a giant of desolate similitude. Surrounded by delicate steel chimneys, belching smoke, and crowned with two Euclidean blue lines, Aylesford Newsprint recycles paper to meet the voracious demand of the late 20th century. On the horizon, the North Downs struggle into view.

By the time cars and coaches reach the large well-surfaced car park, the satanic mills have disappeared behind a screen of trees. Tourists of every creed and colour are welcome to roam the grounds of this historic place, where poverty and abstinence have vanished with the view.

A jovial friar, in dark brown habit and Jesus sandals, offers no begging bowl, but an invitation to explore this prosperous place of prayer. The cloister chapel is warm and inviting behind its great oak door. Soft carpets, a simple stone altar, flickering candles, and the faint smell of incense, give a womb-like feel. Other chapels and shrines are uncluttered with plain walls, bold ceramics and simple statues .

The shrine area is the site of the medieval church which took over fifty years to build, and was then demolished in the 16th century. It was dedicated in 1417 by the Bishop of Rochester. Now the robust complex of the main shrine and four chapels, built between 1958 and 1965, have been made to last. Every surface gleams like the smile of the welcoming friar. The long trestle-tables, like those in the 13th century hall, were once used by the pilgrims on their way to Canterbury. Now they are used by businessmen, Rotarians, students, contemporary pilgrims and those on retreat. A well-equipped conference room bristles with sophisticated technology, and three seminar rooms and a bar have been skilfully integrated into this ancient setting. Guests are comfortably accommodated, at today's prices, in the 16th century houses of the Great Courtyard, where Muscovy ducks snuggle up together, defying their celibate surroundings. A red Ford Fiesta sits like an overblown geranium near the low arched stone portal, a 20th century alien in this medieval space.

Ancient and modern, commerce and Christianity, amalgamate seamlessly beside the peaceful river which glides impassively beneath the buildings of the Great Courtyard.

*A glimpse of the Friars, Aylesford*

# Kit's Coty House

*About a mile to the north, eastward of Aylesford, on an eminence, stands the rude and inexplicable monument of antiquity, called Kit's Coity-House.*

This ancient dolmen still stands on Burham Down, a mile-and-a-half to the north-east of Aylesford. A steep path takes the walker through a belt of woodland for a quarter-of-a-mile, when a sudden parting in the trees reveals what could be a prehistoric bus shelter, standing alone on the draughty hillside. From this prominent position, the neolithic chambered tomb looks over the industrial incontinence of Snodland, where the Medway coils serpent-like through the soft chalk of the North Downs. Rising gently from the river, these green and empty hills give welcome and historic space between the conurbations of Maidstone and the Medway towns. Charles Dickens was among the many who have enjoyed the views from this prehistoric vantage point, and used to picnic here with friends, insisting that they take their litter home with them.

The prehistoric monument is thought to be the site of the battle in 455 between the British king, Vortigern, and the Jutes led by their chiefs, Hengist and Horsa. The irony is that Vortigern, the ruler of the totally isolated former Roman province of Britain, invited the Jutes to fight as mercenaries against the savage Picts and Scots. The Jutes helped Vortigern to subdue the Picts and then, liking the 'excellence of the land', decided to stay. They sent for reinforcements and then fought Vortigern's troops on Burham Down, winning two pitched battles in 455 and 456. Vortigern's son, Catigern, fought hand-to-hand against Horsa, and both men were slain in the combat. This left Hengist and his son, Aesc, as the war-leaders of the Jutes. During the battle, it is said that Hengist raised his standard on a large, white stone and declared himself King of Kent. An isolated ancient stone lies on the hill close to the line of The Pilgrim's Way and is known as 'The White Horse Stone'. According to modern legend, it was by Hengist's defeat that Kent gained its county emblem of the rampant white horse, possibly painted on the sail of the Jute's longship. Cartigern was buried beneath Kit's Coty House, while Horsa, *was buried at a place about four miles distant, denominated*

*Horstead; (probably from the name of the hero) where a number of large stones mark the place of that memorable rencounter.*

Ireland may well have been referring to the fallen group of stones called Little Kit's Coty nearer Aylesford. In any case, by the end of the 5th century, Kent was established as the first of the English kingdoms.

Samuel Ireland's *ingenious* friend, Grose, conjectures in his book, *Antiquities of England and Wales*, that the name of Kit, or Cat, may be short for Catigern; and as there are many similar stones in Cornwall called Coits, *Kit's Coity-House may express Catigern's house, built with Coits.* A neat explanation, but more modern theories state that it comes from the Celtic *Ked-Coit* meaning 'tomb in the woods'. Whatever the origin, these ancient sandstone boulders are a benchmark in English history.

*Kit's Coty House, near Aylesford*

# Allington Castle

*This venerable ruin, though within a few yards of the river, is by the range of trees on its bank, nearly excluded from the view . . . its general situation is so circumscribed, as to render it difficult to select a favourable point . . . The remains of this ancient castle are now used as a farm-house; they are of considerable extent, and many of its external parts are in a tolerable good state of preservation. The moat, or ditch, that surrounds it still exists.*

Two hundred years later the *venerable ruin* remains obscured by trees, surrounded by less venerable motor-cruisers; white aliens in shining armour, visors down, antennae up.

Allington Castle, no longer a ruin, hides in a loop of the Medway, a magic medieval space amongst a web of roads, railways and suburbs. Allington Lock marks the point where the Medway ceases to be tidal. The large concrete weir stretches across the river like an unfinished bridge beside the double lock. A picture postcard Victorian lock-keeper's house sits on the west bank. A large pub beside the towpath is significantly called the Malta Inn, for their pub-sign is a Maltese cross, logo of the Knights Hospitallers. Here the 20th century traveller can leave the car for some waterside refreshment under the willow trees. Nearby, the Museum of Kent Life boasts Britain's last traditional working oast-house and hand-harvested hop garden. Old Dutch barges, their strong bows blown out like the cheeks of well-fed hamsters, sit decorously on the bank: a reminder of the days when these sturdy workhorses linked the Medway with Europe.

Allington, like all Ireland's subjects, is steeped in history. It was one of the 184 manors in Kent given to the infamous Odo, Bishop of Bayeux, William the Conqueror's half-brother. After Odo's rebellion, his lands were confiscated, and Allington was granted to William, Earl Warenne. In Edward I's reign the castle was purchased for £200 by Sir Stephen de Penchester, Constable of Dover Castle. Allington then became one of the seven chief royal castles in Kent. It was acquired by Sir Henry Wyatt in 1492, and remained in the Wyatt family for the next sixty-two years. In Richard III's reign, Sir Henry was incarcerated in the Tower of London for two years because of his Yorkist sympathies. Ireland tells us that the prisoner, . . . *is said to have been wonderfully preserved and fed there by a cat; for which reason he is reported to have been painted with that animal in his arms.* This anecdote is related on the imposing memorial to the Wyatt family in Boxley Church. Happily, Sir Henry was released on the accession of Henry VII, and quickly became a trusted friend of the king who, in 1508, made him privy councillor and guardian of his son.

*Dutch barge at Allington Lock*

Sir Henry's own son, Thomas, was born at Allington Castle in 1503. This handsome young man was responsible for introducing the sonnet from Italy, and Ireland eulogises his literary achievements: *He is called by Anthony Wood 'The Delight of Muses, and of Mankind'; and Leland, in his poem on his death, entitles him 'Incomparabilis'.*

As a young man, Thomas believed in living dangerously, for he formed a close friendship with Anne Boleyn, which continued after his marriage to Elizabeth Brooke, Lord Cobham's daughter. For this friendship, platonic or otherwise, he was imprisoned twice in the Tower of London. The Machiavellian Thomas extracted himself on each occasion, keeping his head literally and metaphorically. He was then sent on a mission to Rome, which was the start of a distinguished diplomatic career.

In 1527, Henry VIII stayed at Allington Castle on his way to meet Cardinal Wolsey who was trying to arrange the king's divorce from Catherine of Aragon. When the attempt failed, Henry made himself head of the English Church and married Anne in 1533. Thomas, now a Privy Councillor, was ewer bearer at Anne Boleyn's coronation. During the years 1527 to 1544, Allington's visitors included Henry VIII, Cardinal Wolsey, Anne Boleyn and Catherine Parr. A charge of 7s and 4d (36 pence) was made for the cost of dining en route for Leeds Castle in October 1544.

Sir Thomas Wyatt the Elder was a wit as well as a poet. He supposedly encouraged Henry VIII to proceed with his divorce of Catherine of Aragon, notwithstanding the opposition of Rome. Ireland takes up the story:

*An invidious, but happy sarcasm of this great man dropt in the willing ear of the succeeding Monarch,* (Henry VIII), *is thought to have been instrumental in promoting the Reformation. He* (Thomas) *observed : "It was a hard thing a man could not repent without the Pope's leave."*

Sir Thomas the Elder died of a fever in October 1542. He was succeeded by his son, Thomas, who, intending to prevent the marriage of Queen Mary to Philip of Spain, led the ill-fated Wyatt Rebellion in 1554. He was executed and forfeited his estates at Allington and Boxley to the Crown. During their glittering years at Allington, the Wyatt family did much to improve and update the castle, changing it from a medieval stronghold to a Tudor house fit for royalty.

Subsequently, Elizabeth I granted Allington on lease to the master of her jewels, John Astley, who later moved to the Archbishop's Palace in Maidstone. In the 18th century, the property was rented by two families, owned by Lord Romney and fell into serious decline. In Ireland's time it was so ruinous that it came close to demolition. In 1905, the castle was rescued by Sir Martin Conway and heavily restored. The final Tudor restoration took place when the Carmelite Friars bought the castle in 1951 from Lord Conway's daughter, Agnes, for £15,000. Like Aylesford, it became available for retreats and seminars and opened to the public until 1991 when it was closed. In 1996, it was sold by the Carmelites to a private buyer who spent two years restoring it to its former glory and now occupies it as a private home. Truly a case of 'an Englishman's home is his castle'.

The secluded castle stands guard over forty acres of beautiful river frontage. Its towers, moat, battlements and turrets make it a fairy tale castle, all the more so because it can only be viewed from afar. The approach down Castle Road is only half-a-mile from the Mid-Kent Shopping Centre and the dreary petticoats of Maidstone. The tarmac narrows sharply and ends abruptly at a barred gatehouse. Allington Lock lies to the left, and a pumping station and a boat yard to the right. Today, the explorer can only gaze with awe at the distant mirage behind a stout wire fence.

*Courtyard in Allington Castle*

# Maidstone

*On the approach to Maidstone the river scenery is pleasingly diversified, by a long range of spreading trees on the bank of the Medway; which, with its venerable stone bridge, and the country contiguous, produce rather an interesting landscape.*

The river banks, along the two-mile stretch of the Medway between Allington and Maidstone, are still surprisingly green. The *liquid serpent* glides past woods and fields, boat yards and sawmills, and under the solid concrete of the M20 bridge, richly decorated in colourful graffiti. The silence is broken by birdsong and the constant roar of motorway traffic. From the trussed steel railway bridge, built in 1927, the river becomes urbanized. The tree-lined banks here are replaced with steel, glass and concrete, neatly trimmed with paved walkways. The Medway now enters the county town of Maidstone, where the barges have departed and the motorcar holds sway.

Arthur Mee describes Maidstone as: 'The great centre-point of Kent, a pivot of its history, the finest town on the Medway, a 20th century hive of life with the 15th century lingering in its streets, Maidstone draws all Kent into it.'

Others who have written about the Medway have not been so kind. Certainly it is a town with a past, famous for rebellions, ragstone and refugees. Ireland omits to mention the famous rebellions by Wat Tyler, Jack Cade or even the Battle of Maidstone in 1648 when the Royalists were defeated by the Parliamentarians in the bloodiest battle of the Civil War.

The port of Maidstone was the centre for quarrying and shipping of ragstone. From the quarries at Boughton Monchelsea, Loose and Tovil, rag went via 'the Wharffe ate the Watr syde', in Maidstone for such prestigious buildings as Hampton Court, Rochester Castle and Bridge, Cooling Castle, Westminster Palace and the Tower of London. Shot for cannons was also quarried here and shipped to forts like Garrison Point, Upnor Castle and the Tower of London.

In Elizabeth I's reign, there was an influx of refugees from the Netherlands. Some of these Dutch immigrants settled in Maidstone and were probably the first nonconformists who worshipped freely. They brought not only their puritanism but also their skills as cloth weavers, which gave both employment and revenue to the indigenous population of Maidstone.

*The central situation of this town renders it highly eligible for the purposes of provincial meetings . . . and public business . . . situated in a delightful vale, happily screened by surrounding hills; and is justly famed for the dryness of its soil and its excellent water.*

Apart from All Saints' Church, Ireland would not have recognized the town. Looking downstream from the Archbishop's Palace, the old 14th century bridge, depicted in his sketch, has been replaced by a solid stone bridge, built in 1879. This was the work of Sir Joseph Bazalgette of London's main drainage fame, and is strong enough to carry the incessant flow of traffic, which pours down the wide High Street and sends pedestrians scuttling into subterranean walkways below, to cross the road in safety.

Maidstone has embraced the 20th century with enthusiasm, haphazardly throwing up an assortment of high-rise concrete, brick, and glass, on the banks of the silent river. A line of old barges on the east bank are all that is left of Maidstone's flourishing water trade. These floating memorabilia provide a rather different place to eat and sleep. The open ironwork of the giant gasometer, downstream from the bridge, occludes the . . . *rich verdure of the adjoining country.*

Ireland admires the principal street, describing it as *spacious, and, from its easy ascent, is kept continually clean and dry*. No doubt, all the dirt was swept down the hill and into the river. In the 18th century, the town was unlit and insanitary. The streets were not paved, lit or drained until 1793, the same year that Ireland was writing his book. The Medway took most of Maidstone's sewage until the construction of separating tanks at Allington in 1880. Gas arrived some twenty-five years later and electricity in 1901.

Ireland tells us that at the end of the 18th century the principal trade was still navigation . . . *by which channel the various productions of this county, its timber from the Wealds and other parts, paper from the neighbouring mills, grain and flour, hops and fruit, are, through this place, circulated to the capital as well as foreign markets.*

*The abundant fertility of the country around, in corn fields, hop and filbert grounds, orchards of apple, cherry, and other fruit trees, not only so far enrich the scenery as to delight the eye of the English traveller, but have induced some foreign writers to denominate it 'The Hungaria of Great Britain.'*

The 'Garden of England' has now shrunk to make way for houses and factories. It is exhaust fumes that fill the air, as cars circulate the town, streaming west from the High Street across Town Bridge, and east across St Peter's Bridge above an empty Medway. From the top of the busy High Street, lined with plate-glass and plastic, there is a good view across the river to the substantial brick-and-slate of an unvenerable supermarket. Bank Street, a pedestrianised backwater, lies beside the High Street, a random assortment of Tudor, Georgian and modern buildings.

Upstream from Town Bridge, Old Father Time has been urged to stand still. The straight, wide Medway here processes passed All Saints' Church and the Archbishop's Palace, much as in Ireland's time:

*The church is situated upon an agreeable eminence, on the eastern bank of the Medway, and is a good specimen of gothic architecture. Its embattlements, and time worn tower, leave little room to regret the loss of the steeple, which is reported to have originally stood here, and which is said to have been destroyed by lightning.*

*The Archbishop's Palace, Maidstone*

The solid stone walls of the 14th century church and palace retain an air of wealth and status today. The Medway glides passed like a protective moat, while the mature trees of the palace gardens give space and dignity to the ancient buildings. Ducks and swans replace the barges and fishing boats of Ireland's time, leaving tiny wakes on the smooth water.

All Saints' Church remains much as it was in 1395, although the north porch was added early in the 20th century. The wooden spire, mentioned by Ireland, was struck by lightning in 1730. It crashed down through the roof of the south aisle and did considerable damage. The tomb of Archbishop Courtney is situated in the chancel, but there is some doubt whether he was in fact interred here, for it was customary to bury Archbishops in Canterbury Cathedral. It seems, therefore, that this archbishop has the dubious privilege of having a tomb in both Canterbury and Maidstone. In his text Ireland voices these doubts, *within the church there is a monument, and some lines on the founder; though it does not appear in Camden, Godwin, &tc. that he was interred here. Weever however seems to think that he was buried under his monument in the chancel.* In his history of Maidstone Parish Church The Reverend Canon Peter S. Naylor, vicar of Maidstone from 1974 to 1991, writes: '. . . during the last years of the 18th century the Maidstone tomb was opened and a body discovered.'

The most striking feature of this homogenous church is its size, and the building itself remains much as it was in 1395. The nave is one of the widest of any English parish church, measuring ninety-three feet (28·3 metres). Originally there would have been no seating in the nave, it was a case of standing-room only. The stone seats along some of the walls were for children, the old and infirm, which gave rise to the saying, 'the weakest go to the wall.'

There are some interesting memorials in the church including one to the Astley family. Allington Castle was granted to John Astley on lease, by Elizabeth I, and later he moved to the Archbishop's Palace next to All Saints' Church. The heraldic crest of the Washington family can be seen near the south door; Laurence Washington died in 1619 and was 'collateral forbear' to President George Washington. The family arms incorporate the Stars and Stripes, on which the American flag was subsequently based.

The medieval Archbishop's Palace was originally an irregular range of buildings set round a large courtyard, bounded by the Medway and the Len to the west and north, All Saints' Church to the south, and the archbishop's stables to the east. Today, the courtyard is a public garden, the medieval gatehouse a tourist office, and the archbishop's stables a carriage museum.

The Manor of Maidstone was held by Archbishops of Canterbury before the Domesday survey. In 1207, the wealthy William de Cornhill, rector of St Mary's, Maidstone, gave his house to the archbishops for their own use. Little remains of the original house, but it was rebuilt as a palace by Archbishop Ufford in 1348, and soon extended to form part of a series of palaces used by archbishops travelling round their diocese. At the Reformation, it was ceded to the Crown, and in 1580 sold to Sir John Astley, Master of the Queen's Jewels. The new owner refronted the main palace building in the Elizabethan style.

Today, the palace itself is a venue for every type of function: weddings, christenings, exhibitions and concerts to name but a few. Archbishop Ufford, might have been surprised to see his palace being used as the venue for a Psychic Fayre in 1998, but would have been happy to know that it has been carefully restored and preserved. Visitors are welcome to view the old building, use facilities fit for any archbishop, and refresh themselves in one of the grand reception rooms whose large mullioned windows look out over the river to the Lockmeadow Leisure Complex. Currently under construction, and flooding the west bank with bricks and mortar, this building will house cinemas, an entertainment centre, a nightclub, and five restaurants. In addition, there will be an open and covered market and an agricultural hall. Samuel Ireland and the archbishops would possibly not have given it their seal of approval.

The old college beside All Saints' Church has changed little. The ancient buildings were presented to Maidstone Borough Council by Sir Garrard Tyrwhitt-Drake JP, DC, to mark the 4th centenary of the granting of the Charter to Maidstone in the 12th mayorality of the borough, 1949-1956. The Kentish ragstone building sits quietly beside the churchyard, like a bewildered old man at the end of his days. It is now used by the Kent Music School.

\* \* \* \* \*

*In the country about Maidstone, now almost covered with hops, this plant is said to have been first cultivated . . . at the period of the Reformation . . . Scenes, such as we have described hold out invitations not to be resisted by the wealthy and the great. The hills and valleys around, covered with villas and mansion houses, confirm the truth of the representation given.*

One of the great mansions built here was, *Lord Romney's ancient seat, called the Mote, about a mile to the east of the town, though not in appearance a stately mansion, has yet within it many elegant and stately apartments: in park scenery, the hand of nature, with little assistance from art, has been evidently lavish.*

No more is mentioned of this historic park called the Mote, from the Anglo-Saxon word 'mot' meaning a gathering place. The mansion Ireland refers to was pulled down in 1799 and the present house, built for Lord Romney and designed by Daniel Asher Alexander (later responsible for Maidstone and Dartmoor prisons), was built between 1793 and 1800. Mote Park's chief claim to fame came on 1 August 1799, when Lord Romney, the lord-lieutenant of the county, invited twenty-two companies of West Kent Volunteers to muster in the park to be reviewed by George III and entertained by his lordship. This force numbered about 5,500 Volunteers from forty-two settlements, and the occasion was attended by many of the great and the good including the Prime Minister, William Pitt, and the Duke of York. A gigantic feast followed this loyal display, and seven-and-a-half miles of timber were required to make the tables. Maidstone entertained 20,000 visitors, East Lane was renamed King Street and fireworks were set off in Fairmeadow. All this would surely have gladdened the heart of Samuel Ireland. Two years later in 1801, a pavilion was erected by the Volunteers in Mote Park to commemorate this epic review.

Mote House, now a rather crumbling edifice, sits on its hill overlooking the great artificial lake which nestles into a wooded and undulating landscape. Until recently it was used as a Cheshire Home and is currently owned by the Borough Council. Across this sheet of water, the commemorative pavilion, a migrated Greek temple, eyeballs the big house. The River Len, from Leeds Castle to the Medway, winds its way quietly passed pedestrians, cyclists and dogs, before emptying into the great lake. In 1857, the Mote Cricket Club was founded, and famous names like Colin Cowdrey and Frank Woolley have played in county cricket matches at Mote Park.

Before leaving Maidstone, Ireland mentions the *celebrated Pinnenden Heath, which has been a place of considerable note ever since the Conquest.* This historic heath, situated about a mile to the north-east of the town, has shrunk to a recreation ground staked out with lime trees. Yet this has been the place for meetings and courts from earliest times, and the name Penenden signifies in Saxon, a 'place of penalty'. In 1070, a famous court met on this heath when Odo, the greedy and avaricious Bishop of Bayeux, *was charged with having defrauded the See of Canterbury of manors, Lands, and liberties. The trial lasted three days; and the charge was so clearly proved, as to enable the Archbishop to recover from his false brother, and father of the church, several of his ancient possessions, and to ascertain other matters that were in dispute between the church and king.* Archbishop Lanfranc won the day and Odo turned his attention elsewhere. After William's death, Odo tried to reclaim his lands, but was finally banished for raising a rebellion against King William Rufus. Sheriffs held shire courts on Penenden Heath until the late 1700s.

It was on this heath in 1381, that Wat Tyler was elected to lead the Peasant's Revolt. In 1450 Jack Cade headed a further rebellion by "Kentish Men" who felt aggrieved by heavy taxation and the king's administration. Both these uprisings failed. In 1554, Thomas Wyatt organized an insurrection against the marriage of Queen Mary to Prince Philip of Spain. Wyatt rallied a force of 1,500 men on Penenden Heath and marched on London, but his attempt also failed, and he was beheaded on Tower Hill the same year. On 25 October 1643, during the Civil War, Maidstone received a letter ordering trained soldiers and volunteers, on horse and foot, to assemble at Penenden Heath. After the Parliamentary Reform Act in 1832, county votes were cast in a small shed on the north side of the heath until 1877. Today, it seems incredible that this quiet suburban recreation ground with its poop scoops and parked cars, can have been the touchstone and assembly point for such turbulent events.

The River Len, after leaving Mote Park, joins the Medway just above the Archbishop's Palace in Maidstone. Here, the Medway, unperturbed by old and new, flows steadily on, curving westwards in a right-angled bend metamorphosing in an instant from urban to rural. The gardens of substantial 20th century houses sweep down to the river, willows weep on manicured lawns and polished daffodils brighten the banks. A line of trees obscures Maidstone's industrial estate, as the towpath passes along wooded banks fringed with dull vegetation. A moment's sunlight can turn them into the rich green of a tropical rain forest, mirrored on the river's back. The occasional roar of electric trains disturbs the peace.

Of Tovil, Samuel Ireland writes:

*About a mile out of town* (Maidstone), *at the pleasant village of Tovil, on an eminence, commanding an extensive and beautiful view, the Anabaptists have chosen a spot in a rocky and romantic situation, as a burial place for their fraternity. Its elevation and distance from the river, seem to indicate, that, however fond they may have been of emerging in water, when living, they are determined to keep at a distance from that element in the stage beyond this life.*

In the 17th century, the Anabaptists had a meeting house at Tovil and were given a little burial-ground on the south side of the village. As dissenters, they were persecuted and harassed until the Act of Toleration in 1672. Ireland's humorous observation indicates that he had little time for either papists or nonconformists.

This *pleasant village* has been subsumed by Maidstone. Now it appears an amorphous mass of tightly-packed houses, light industry, and a recycling centre, with Church Street leading to a litter-strewn graveyard of drunken tombstones without a church. Burial Ground Lane and The Royal Paper Mill public house give clues to the village's history. The *extensive* view is mainly of Maidstone's drab architecture clinging to the hills, a little less *beautiful* than in Ireland's time. Bydews Place, a Wealden hall house refronted in the 18th century, survives down by the river. Upstream, a trussed steel bridge crosses the Medway, replacing the 1886 goods line to Tovil.

The Medway, from Maidstone to Tonbridge, is a stretch of the river that Ireland would recognise if he either walked the towpath or sat in the train. Situated on the north bank and keeping faithfully to the river, the railway gives the traveller unspoiled views of the Medway, flowing gently through undulating countryside. Perched on the embankment, roads and cars are invisible, and the Kentish ragstone bridges of East Farleigh and Teston have changed little since Ireland sketched them. The fertile slopes still retain hops, oast-houses and orchards; wild flowers grow in profusion along the river banks, and the river still *wears an appearance equal to that of a garden in its highest state of cultivation.* Two hundred years on, Ireland's quotation is still apposite: *'The silver Medway glides, and on her breast / Reflects the varied landscape'.*

Plate XVII

Nettlestead Church

Plate XVIII

Twyford Bridge

Plate XIX

Tonbridge

Plate XX

Hever Castle

# Boxley Abbey

*Boxley Abbey is situated a little to the eastward of Pinnenden Heath, and was formerly part of the vast possessions of the pious Bishop of Baieux.*

After this sarcastic comment about Odo, the infamous Bishop of Bayeux, Ireland gives vent to his feelings about all things popish. The abbey, founded in 1146 by William de Ypres, Earl of Kent, was favoured by royalty and became rich and important. Ireland expresses his disapproval very frankly:

*Edward I granted to the Abbot of Boxley many privileges and immunities . . . Our senate, at a succeeding period, we find either to have been greatly overstocked with these dignitaries, there being no less within its walls at that time than sixty-four abbots, and thirty-six priors, or, if their property gave them place there, our common wealth was most grievously over-run by a race of lazy and impoverishing caterpillars.*

Boxley is remembered today as a place of ecclesiastical fraud. Ireland enjoys telling the story:

*The abbey was formerly much famed for a wooden figure, called the Rood of Grace, the work of a needy carpenter, with which the priests for a long time deluded their credulous and silly followers, till the knavery being detected, the idol was defaced.*

The 'needy carpenter' had made an ingenious crucifix with a head that bowed, mouth that opened and eyes that rolled. It attracted hundreds of pilgrims, smiling benignly when the offerings were large, and scowling ferociously when they were small. During the sacking of the monasteries, Henry VIII's commissioners found old wire and rotten sticks at the back of the mechanism which tricked many *credulous* pilgrims. The wonder-working piece of propaganda was then triumphantly displayed in Maidstone marketplace, before being taken to St Paul's in London, and publicly burned.

Henry VIII gave Boxley Abbey and the Manor to the Wyatts of Allington, with which family they remained until 1793 when they passed to Lord Romney.

Boxley is now a private house, tucked peacefully into the few remaining abbey walls. In 1720, the Best family, wealthy brewers from Chatham, bought property in Boxley village and later acquired more land to the west which included the abbey. Seven generations of Bests lived at Park House, Boxley. In 1951, when the last of the Bests died, the abbey passed to a nephew, Sir John Shaw, the 9th Baronet of Eltham. Sir John Shaw assumed, by Royal Licence, the name and arms of Best in addition to his own. By this time, wars and death duties had forced the sale of substantial parts of the estates, but the Best-Shaws were able to keep the abbey intact with the tithe barn, and the seventeen acres of land enclosed within the abbey walls.

In 1810, a fire destroyed a large part of the substantial house. Today, the remaining mellow brick-and-stone wing makes a manageable and dignified home in the grounds of the ancient abbey. The natural garden is a place of peace, where each generation seems to have added something of itself. A wide variety of shrubs clamber over the old walls, bluebells and cow-parsley blend happily with herbaceous plants, roses and clipped yews. A large cedar spreads its great branches over the green lawn, and the walled garden by the house is bright with formal flower beds. A great terrace was built on the ruins of the monk's church, wide enough to be used as a bowling green in Victorian times. Today, an ancient oak, which could have been a sapling when the chapel was destroyed, rises like a phoenix from the ruins, and clumps of primroses grow in the rough grass under the mature trees. The view of lush, green fields stretching to the steep chalk Downs cannot have changed much since the times when monks tended gillyflowers and roses in the garden. The old boundary walls, thatched with vigorous ivy, are still visible, but powerless to protect this gentle place from the 20th century. The invader, today, is the incessant roar of traffic from the M20. Soon, the high-speed Channel Tunnel rail link will add its share of metallic decibels to a place where once, the only sounds were plainsong chants, and the regular toll of bells.

The Kentish ragstone tithe barn stands near the house. This ancient building, two hundred feet (60·959 metres) in length, is said to be the longest in the country, a measure of the importance of the original Cistercian abbey. Although empty for many years, it has changed little over the centuries. The massive 13th century timbers of the long roof, an unending line of crossed swords, are in good condition, and the roof was partly re-tiled after the great storm of 1987.

The barn is divided into two huge sections, with a dividing wall that leans with the prevailing wind. Seven years ago, English Heritage approved the barn's conversion into a business centre, but the plan was abandoned as the £2,000,000 cost of conversion could not be guaranteed. Apart from the ghosts of history, the only occupants today are a few sheep, some pigeons and the wind.

Although Boxley is best remembered for the greedy 'miracles', it is easy to forget that, for 400 years, the monks devoted their lives to peace and prayer. They also provided local people with shelter, education and a place to work, as well as giving hospitality to the many pilgrims. In spite of the invasive roar of the 20th century, a feeling of spirituality endures in this very English oasis.

# Leeds Castle

*Leeds Castle was anciently part of those possessions lavishly bestowed by William the Conqueror on his brother Odo, Bishop of Baieux . . . The immense strength of this place induced our Monarchs, at all times, to look upon it with an eye of jealousy; and though it was frequently granted to several great families in this country, it has as often, by attainder or escheat, come again into the hands of the Crown.*

*That noble and extensive edifice*, Leeds Castle, lies three miles south-east of Maidstone on the River Len. This seemingly insignificant little river which joins the Medway at All Saints' Church, Maidstone, is full of surprises.

Leeds is a magical castle. The warm sandstone walls float on the calm waters of a great lake, the clear reflection heightening the illusion. Broad acres of undulating Kent countryside surround the dream. The River Len divides into many natural streams, which have been landscaped to enhance the woods and parkland of the estate. Another lake, complete with waterfall staircase, makes a natural breeding habitat for many varieties of duck and waterfowl, from Chinese geese to pochard and black swans. Peacocks and pheasants saunter across acres of manicured grass, posing for eager cameras.

The castle's history goes back 900 years. In 1090, the deceitful Odo was exiled and the king then gave Leeds Castle to his cousin, Hamon de Crevecoeur, who had fought with him at the Battle of Hastings. In 1119, Robert de Crevecoeur started building the stone castle and Leeds Priory, which became one of the richest in Kent, giving hospitality to pilgrims on their way to Canterbury. The de Crevecoeurs ruled over Leeds Castle and the Priory for 200 years after the Norman Conquest.

In 1278, the castle was conveyed to Edward I and his queen, Eleanor of Castile. This devoted couple loved the place, and Edward extended the castle's defences and decided to leave it to his queen as a dower. Although Eleanor died too young to inherit the castle for her widowhood, the tradition of the king granting the castle as dower to his queen had begun, and so the royal ownership of Leeds became a ladies' castle. The last queen to own the property personally was Catherine de Valois, queen of Henry V. She received the castle in 1422, repaired the hall and other buildings, and installed the castle's bell and clock, supposedly one of the oldest in the country. It still strikes the hours today, and was rung when Queen Elizabeth II visited Leeds Castle in March 1981.

Samuel Ireland complains that he was not permitted access . . . *with the pleasing expectation of innocently gratifying himself, and perhaps affording no irrational amusement to others, by the display of the beauties of art and nature, with which this quarter of our island is enriched . . . all access was barred; no approaches were suffered.*

He concludes his history and description of the castle with a rather unkind anecdote about the Fairfax family, who owned the castle at the end of the 17th century . . . *recording an aged Lady Fairfax, in the time of the celebrated Dean of St. Patrick . . . The Old Lady hearing that Swift was walking round the castle, and imagining he would be gratified with an interior view of it, politely sent him an invitation for that purpose, to which we are told the churl, with as little of point as of civility, brutally replied, 'tell your Lady I came here to see old walls, not old women.'*

In Ireland's time, Leeds Castle belonged to Robert Fairfax, who was MP for Maidstone and Kent. Under his ownership, *Gothick improvements* were made, emulating Horace Walpole's Strawberry Hill. In 1778, Robert Fairfax welcomed King George III and Queen Charlotte to the castle while they were reviewing troops encamped nearby at Maidstone. At Fairfax's death in 1793 (the year Ireland published his *Picturesque Scenes on the River Medway*), the property passed to his nephew, Denny Martin. In the 1820s, Fiennes Wykeham-Martin spent vast sums of money restoring the castle's medieval style and it has changed little in appearance since. One hundred years later, the castle was bought by Lady Baillie who set about its restoration, inside and out, with imagination, vigour and cash; embellishing Leeds Castle became her life's work. She created the warmth and classic elegance of the interior we see today, designed the Wood Garden bordered by little streams of the River Len, and brought rare birds from all over the world for the garden and lakes. She lived at Leeds longer than any other owner in its recorded history, and her work for the castle ranks with Edward I and Eleanor of Castile, Edward III, Henry VIII, and Fiennes Wykeham-Martin.

Between the two World Wars, Leeds Castle became a dazzling centre of hospitality, entertaining royalty from home and abroad. During the Second World War, the Petroleum Warfare Department was directed from Leeds, developing flame-throwing weapons in case of invasion. When this crisis passed, Lady Baillie permitted the castle to be used as a military hospital and convalescent home for badly burned pilots.

After the war, Lady Baillie lived a quiet family life and set about preserving Leeds Castle for posterity. When she died in 1974, she gave the castle to the nation in perpetuity, not just as a lifeless monument, but as the home of active charitable work. She arranged that, besides being open for the public to enjoy, it should be used as a centre for international medical seminars. To achieve this, she established the Leeds Castle Foundation as a charitable trust.

Today, the public can view the castle and grounds all year round. The trustees have continued to improve amenities at the castle, without spoiling its fairy tale quality. The barbican and fortified mill, built by Odo, Bishop of Bayeux, were restored in 1985-1989, a feature that would interest Mr Ireland, as would the Norman cellars, filled with bottles of wine, many from the estate's own vineyard, (replanted on the site of the original vineyard mentioned in the Domesday Book). The rooms are warm and inviting, the ceilings adorned with beautifully carved beams, many brought over from Normandy by Lady Baillie. Bright silks hang from the walls, and gas logs flicker cheerfully in the ancient fireplaces. The rooms of the gloriette are carpeted and lavishly furnished, their large mullioned windows looking across the lake to the undulating countryside and the long natural wall of the North Downs.

There is a sense of continuity and security within these thick walls. The long dining table in the Henry VIII Banqueting Hall is laid ready for the next guests, the cushions in the drawing-rooms plumped ready for the next diplomat or medical researcher. In the 1990s the castle is multi-functional, hosting international conferences, firework displays, food and wine festivals, concerts and balloon fiestas. The Fairfax Hall, with its high-timbered roof, serves food from snacks to three-course lunches, and smarter meals are also available in the Terrace Room. A golf-course and shop give additional pleasure and income.

The castle exudes the best of British private enterprise. Historically, it has been a symbol of power and status on the road to Europe. At the end of the 20th century, commercially, it remains a status symbol. Thousands of foreigners visit the castle annually, and medical researchers from many parts of the world attend the seminars. International summit conferences have been held at Leeds Castle, the latest being the 1998 G8 Environment Ministers' Conference. The patriotic Samuel Ireland should have been happy with that, even though he might not have been so pleased to see swarms of foreigners invading this picturesque corner of British history.

*Leeds Castle from the east*

# East Farleigh

East Farleigh remains a picturesque scene. The medieval bridge was recorded in 1324 when an inquisition was held to discover who was responsible for its upkeep. It is only 11' 6" wide (3·5 metres) and has no refuges for pedestrians. It was over this bridge that General Fairfax brought his troops when he attacked the Royalist forces in Maidstone. A simple canopied cross on the bridge denotes the death in September 1849 of 43 'strangers'. It is assumed they were hop-pickers who died of cholera. The 1860 Egyptian-style waterworks on the north bank is now a print firm, and the weather-boarded signal-box and original level-crossing, still in use, sit in a 19th century time warp. The forlorn station buildings stand empty, waiting to be resurrected or demolished. The railway, which once took so much trade from the river has, in turn, lost its trade to the roads. Upstream, the church and oast-houses still stand on the rising ground as they did in Ireland's sketch, but downstream, the metal weir is a 20th century intrusion. White fibreglass motor-cruisers have replaced the wooden sailing-boats and barges of Ireland's day.

*East Farleigh station*

# Barming Bridge

*Across the stream a small wooden bridge, over which the 'lowing herd' are passing to their homes; and the lofty spire of Barming, richly whitening in the distance.*

Ireland sketches a small wooden bridge at Barming, also known as Kettle Bridge or St Helen's. It was replaced in 1996 by a less romantic steel and concrete structure. The scene, however, is still peaceful. Barming village is a mix of old and new with ribbons of 20th century buildings lining the busy Maidstone road, while the older houses trickle down the steep hill to the river. The *decent church, that tops the neighbouring hill,* still sits aloof among the fields with a perfect view of the river and the green slopes on the other side.

*Nature has been no less bountiful to this place in other and more essential particulars: its soil produces a great quantity of what is called Kentish Rag Stone, which affords particular nourishment to the root of the hop, and the land is consequently very productive in the growth of that useful plant.*

There are fewer signs of that *useful plant* today, but this stretch of the river emanates peace and tranquillity. In midsummer the giant hogweed dominates the river banks, a crowd of white parasols stretching for the sky.

At this point, Mr Ireland, moved by the beauty around him, quotes some lines from Christopher Smart, a poet born in 1726 at Shipbourne: *. . . so energetic was his piety, and so commanding his eloquence, . . . no lover of the beauties of Nature and Poetry can, I trust, refuse to be carried along with him when he exclaims:*

'What are the tow'rs,
The work of lab'ring man and clumsy art . . .
Thou idiot that asserts, there is not God,
View and be dumb for ever————
Go bid Vitruvius or Palladio build
The bee his mansion, or the ant her cave-
Go call Corregio, or let Titian come
To paint the hawthorn's bloom, or teach the cherry
To blush with just vermillion. '

# Teston Bridge

*To the west of Barming, on a noble ascent from the Medway, stands Teston House, the mansion of Mrs Bouverie; the extensive and diversified scenery which surrounds it, and the beautiful meandring stream beneath, highly enriched by its elegant stone bridge, afford an enchanting combination of objects.*

Teston's *elegant stone bridge* remains the least altered of the Medway's four medieval ragstone bridges. Cradled between sloping green banks, softened with woodland, the mellow stones of this 15th century bridge straddle the river with easy grace. The original seven arches have been reduced to six, with the large, pointed centre arch being rebuilt in 1793 to improve navigation, and one of the four flood arches being removed during repairs in 1830. Ireland comments on these points:

*the bridge, though lofty, is yet often impassable, from the sudden overflowing of the river, which here frequently rises eighteen feet above its usual surface in the course of twenty-four hours, and as suddenly falls again to its natural level.*

Flooding is just as likely to happen today, but can be controlled both by the lock sluices and the flood barrier in Haysden Park, Tonbridge.

To the stranger, nothing is what is seems. Teston is pronounced Teeson, for the story goes that the sign-writer for the South Eastern Railway Company, omitted the middle t, no doubt imitating the way locals pronounced it. The Railway Company refused to change his sign, and the village became known as Teeson.

Barham Court, formally known as Teston House, reverted to its original name when Mrs Bouverie died in 1799. Conspicuously sited on the north bank of the river, overlooking a stretch of fertile green landscape, this great mansion flaunts all the classical confidence of the Age of Enlightenment. In 1793, Ireland tells us that the house had recently undergone *such liberal improvements and additions, as to give it the air of a new edifice.* He was not entirely happy about these improvements, preferring the *varied and intersected parts and ornaments of the ancient style . . . at all times, more grateful to the eye than the square front, and as regularly disposed square windows of a modern erection.*

Edward Hasted, the 18th century historian, described Barham Court as *the greatest ornament in this part of the country.* Samuel Ireland, with a little artistic licence, includes the house in his sketch.

The original name, Barham, comes from the Bearham family, whose Norman name was Fitz Urse signifying 'son of a bear'. Randal Fitz Urse goes down in history as being one of the four knights who slew Thomas à Becket at Canterbury Cathedral in 1170. Once again quoting Hasted, Samuel Ireland takes up the story of the estate and the pedigree of its owners.

*Of this stock was the famous Nicholas Barham, Serjeant at Law in the reign of Elizabeth, from whose family this manor descended to the Botelers: it afterwards, on division of the property, came by device to the present owner, Mrs Bouverie, who is related to the Earl Radnor.*

Mrs Bouverie set about modernising and enlarging the house, giving it the *square front and regularly disposed windows* thought by Ireland to be inappropriate in such picturesque scenery. The architect, Benjamin Latrobe, like so many of his contemporaries, following the 18th century philosophy, believed that all Nature was a garden. The great arched windows on the south side have a magnificent view of the rising ground across the Medway to orchards and hop-gardens, oast-houses and lush, green fields. In 1796, Latrobe went to America where he influenced the development of the neoclassical architectural style throughout the nation. He helped to rebuild Washington after the war of 1814, and added the entrance portico to the White House.

Sir Charles Middleton, Admiral of the Fleet until 1805 when he became Lord Barham, was reputedly the first to receive the signal of England's victory at the Battle of Trafalgar at Barham Court. His naval chaplain, James Ramsey, became vicar of Teston Church in 1781. Both James Ramsey and Lord Barham, witnessed the cruel treatment of slaves in their days with the Fleet, and together they did much to bring about the abolition of slavery.

On 27 May, 1932, a fire destroyed much of Barham Court, but the house was swiftly rebuilt by Sir Herbert Baker. This eminent architect was responsible for many prestigious government buildings, at home and abroad, before the decline of the British Empire. He made extensive alterations to the second storey and the interior, and the house has changed little since then. Barham Court treasures were auctioned in 1975, raising a sum of £100,000. In 1998, the freshly-painted mansion is now used as a business centre, while the more modest stable block has been converted into twenty-eight attractive apartments. All who live or work there have a rare view of the old stone bridge in its unspoiled 'Garden of England'.

# Wateringbury

*About a mile-and-a-half above Teston we pass Watringbury, called, in the Textus Roffensis, Wotringaberia; a name probably derived from its low and watery situation.*

The station, a marina, a pub, and a busy road are situated in the low and watery part of the village. The church, which Ireland felt was worthy of mention, stands on higher ground, along with some mellow, red brick 18th century houses, lining a pleasant street.

*The manor was anciently in the possession of the Bishop of Baieux,* (there was very little that was not) . . . *is now the property of Sir Thomas Stiles, Baronet, to whose family a handsome pyramidical monument is erected in the church-yard.*

Ireland fails to mention the handsome monument to Charles I's cupbearer, Oliver Style, and his wife, situated inside the church, which is much more striking than the curious Dumb Borsholder of Chart. This is the name given to a black staff of wood about one metre in length with an iron ring and a spike which was the symbol of authority in Saxon courts. This truncheon-like relic once empowered its annually elected keeper to collect one penny from every house in the local hamlet of Pizein Well. In a Saxon-type neighbourhood watch, the Borsholder's keeper was also allowed to smash down the door of any householder suspected of having stolen goods. At official functions, the wooden staff was stood erect, with its door-smashing iron spike thrust into the ground. Quoting from Hasted, Ireland describes and draws the object of this ancient custom, which today perches inconspicuously above the east window of a side-chapel.

An old yew hugs the church porch with a sinister iron chain trapped in the branches. Leaning tombstones lie among the primroses of the grassy churchyard, where the remains of the last Borsholder, Thomas Clampard, a blacksmith, rest in peace. He collected his last penny in 1748. His epitaph may not have been sufficiently elevated for Ireland's book, but says it all:

My sledge and anvil I've declined;
My bellows too have lost their wind;
My fire's extinct, my forge decayed,
And in the dust my vice is laid;
My coals are spent, my iron's gone,
My nails are drove, my work is done.

# Mereworth Castle

*A few miles westward is Mereworth house: it is watered by a small stream that empties itself into our gentle river, and has also, from the beauty of its situation, ample claim to our attention.*

Now known as Mereworth Castle, (pronounced Merryworth), this Palladian villa has a fine pedigree. Built by Colin Campbell for John Fane in 1723, it was modelled on Palladio's Villa Capra outside Venice. Colin Campbell was later asked to design Burlington House in Piccadilly.

Ireland describes Palladio as *deservedly pre-eminent in the list of architects,* and Colin Campbell *seems to have displayed taste and good sense in selecting from the best masters.*

The Palladian extravaganza was built on the site of an old moated manor, with the moat being retained until the 19th century. The cost, in the 18th century, was £100,000 including the grounds. This princely sum justified demolishing the existing village and church in 1746 to make way for the castle. In 1779, the old rectory followed suit as it obstructed the view.

The ninety-feet (27·432 metres) square building has a circular salon in the centre, and each front . . . *a handsome portico of the Ionic order: the grand facade is by a very noble flight of steps. The building is crowned with a semicircular dome of timber, covered with lead . . . beneath the two domes are twenty-four funnels that convey smoak to the lantern above, which is finished with copper.* The owner, John Fane, inherited the Earldom of Westmorland in 1736 and wanted a house fitting his new social status. The inception of a sophisticated Italianate villa, surrounded by a moat and set among Kentish hop-fields, must have presented something of the shock of the new to Ireland and his contemporaries. The anomalous extravaganza was the result of the enthusiasm of Campbell and Fane.

In 1968, the castle was sold to William Robinson for £200,000, which seems cheap at the price for six hundred acres, four lakes, six cottages and a hundred acre stud farm. This sophisticated house was the setting for the film of Ian Fleming's *Casino Royale,* where James Bond plays baccarat for high stakes to outwit his opponent. The Robinsons created a beautiful garden in this Kentish Eden, and produced exotic fruit such as twirly bananas. However, in the 1970s, feeling the need to add to his growing collection of mansions, His Excellency Sayed Mohamed Mahdi Al-Tajir, Ambassador of the United Arab Emirates, bought the castle for £500,000. Much to the chagrin of garden-lovers, His Excellency has not shared the Robinsons' enthusiasm for horticultural exotica.

The great house sits back from the road, a blushing Italian aristocrat far from home. On the entrance gates, the lion of Venice has been replaced by a German Shepherd. Inside, the building reflects the spirit of the age where an exuberance of baroque stucco and gilt, mythology and Venetian frivolity, are depicted within the classical proportions of a dazzling house that is also a home.

*Mereworth Castle*

# Nettlestead Place

*The grand entrance to the ancient place-house of Nettlestead, as it appears in the annexed view, is yet standing; and the uncouth mixture of Gothic and Grecian therein discernible, denotes it to have been erected about the beginning of the seventeenth century, a period famed for its absurdity and tasteless ornaments in building.*

Nettlestead or Nedestede, was included in the Domesday Book. The inauspicious name is thought to mean, 'the place where nettles grow'; certainly they were thriving at the end of the 18th century when Ireland writes that Nettlestead Place was overrun with weeds and shrubs, and the great hall was being used for drying hops. There may once have been a ford over the Medway at this point, and possibly a Roman road by way of this ford from Coxheath to Otford. More recently, it was thought to be the 'Smallbridge Manor' of Northcote Parkinson's fictional biography of Admiral Lord Hornblower.

*Nettlestead Place*

The *grand entrance,* so strangely portrayed in Ireland's sketch, has vanished. Now a restored manor house, with 20th century extensions, it is framed by a 14th century stone gatehouse, which perches above the drive like an authentic stage set. Lines of chunky, trimmed yews soften the tarmac, and wild and formal gardens, with streams and fishponds, have uninterrupted glimpses of the Medway.

In 1793, the scene, as described by Ireland from Hasted's *History of the County of Kent*, was very different, *bearing . . . every mark of that vicissitude and ruin, the inevitable lot of all the transitory labors of the hand of man which however magnificent, and though supported by pillars of marble,*

'Shall yet decay e'en as the moth's frail cell,

Or sheds of reeds, which summer's heat repell'.

    Ireland gives a brief history of this *transitory labor.* From Norman times the manor was owned by the de Pympe family. Early in the 15th century, Reginald de Pympe was responsible for rebuilding the ancient church and Nettlestead Place. In the 16th century, it descended to the Scott family. An interesting anecdote, not recorded by Samuel Ireland or Edward Hasted, tells of marital disharmony in 1646, between Sir John Scott's unattractive son, Edward, and his wife, Lady Catherine, formerly a daughter of the de Pympe family. This beautiful lady forcibly took possession of the house, and the 'Siege of Nettlestead' ensued when Sir John attempted to starve his wife out. Charles Igglesden in volume XI of his book, *A Saunter Through Kent*, tells us that the lady was secretly fed by a faithful servant; to pass the time she picked out the mortar between the stones of the walls and found hidden treasure. When her husband heard of her discovery, he had the grace to release her.

    It seems that, in the 17th century, nettles once more thrived at the Place, which fell into decay. Early in the 18th century, Ireland tells us that it was alienated to Sir Philip Boteler of Teston, Baronet, and passed via his wife to Mrs Bouverie of Teston House. A manuscript written in 1775 records subsequent piecemeal destruction of the old house: 'The Place, deserted by the family and repairs neglected, is in a ruinous condition.'

    It remained in this state until 1922, when it was purchased by a Mr Vinson who restored it to its former glory. Prior to this, the last occupants were Richard Mears and his mother, who had been nurse to the late Sir Philip Boteler.

In 1977, the property was sold to Mr Roy Tucker, who has lavished time and money on creating a beautiful terraced garden, set among cornfields and hop-gardens, with the river curving gently through the valley beneath; a *picturesque view* that would rival any 18th century watercolour. Only the scenic railway line, running unobtrusively beside the river, hints at the technology that was to come. There is certainly not a nettle to be seen today. The interior of the house has also been beautifully restored and modernised, retaining many of the original features. The fine vaulted 13th century undercroft is in pristine condition, and it is not hard to imagine the knights of old sitting round a table in front of the huge stone fire-place. The adjoining study dates from about 1420, and the mullioned windows of the room above, re-fenestrated in 1580, have views over the lake and gardens to the Medway beyond.

The little 15th century church stands near the big house, tucked well back from the road on a public footpath which leads down to the river. It is a very peaceful place, surrounded by yew trees and old walls. The little ragstone tower survives from the earlier church, but Reginald de Pympe inserted six huge windows into his updated perpendicular-style nave to show off the stained glass of the period. Although some of the original glass still remains, the east window was smashed during the Reformation, and hailstones in the Great Storm of 1763 destroyed the glass on the south side.

On each side of the chancel, well-preserved mural monuments commemorate the two beautiful wives of Sir John Scott. Lady Elizabeth Scott, who died in 1598, came from the great Stafford family, and her father's first wife was none other than Anne Boleyn's sister, Mary. Lady Catherine Scott, who died in 1616, had connections with Penshurst Place and Leeds Castle.

Ireland goes on to describe the oast, or kiln, and the process of drying hops in the 18th century:

*This is done by spreading them on a hair cloth, about twelve feet square, beneath which, at a distance of about eight feet, is a thick plate of iron, regularly heated from below by a spacious stove.*

*The hops lie in this state generally about twelve hours, before they are sufficiently dried, and the quantity of coals or coke consumed in this operation is about a hundred bushels.*

*The hops, thus dried, are put into bags and pressed down by a man, who continues treading on them for that purpose.*

This was all taking place in one of the 'Gothic' staterooms, and a fascinated Ireland drew a sketch and describes the scene with unaccustomed candour:

*The floor of this ancient room of state, deeply covered with hops, and in the midst of it a rustic, half buried in a sack treading them down, in a kind of perpetual motion, as if bit by a tarantula, or troubled with St. Vitus's dance.*

# Twyford Bridge

*We now approach the ancient bridge of Twyford, which is built of stone, and has more of utility than ornament in its construction.*

This bridge links Yalding and East Peckham, crossing the Medway and its tributary, the Teise. The earliest record of its existence is in 1325, when an inquisition was held to discover who was responsible for repairs.

From Ireland's description, the bridge is instantly recognisable:

*The arches are Gothic, with strong angular buttresses raised against the piers, and are carried to the upper part of the side-walls.*

Today, this Kentish ragstone bridge is both ornamental and useful. With the carriageway, 12 feet wide (4·25 metres) between the parapets, there is only room for one row of cars. Part of it collapsed in 1939 and the thin red line across the top is a brick parapet added in 1980. This attractive chunky bridge, with its sharp-pointed cut-waters, has escaped the fate of many ancient bridges which were rebuilt to allow the passage of barge traffic when the river became navigable in the 18th century. The Medway's sinuous loop at Yalding meant that the Navigation Company was able to make a canal, which short-cuts the bend, resulting in Hampstead Lane Lock, with a weir by the bridge. River traffic uses this canal, leaving the river below Twyford Bridge the undisturbed backwater of Ireland's day. Canoeists wait patiently between the weir and the bridge for the sluice-gates to open, when they enjoy a shot of adrenaline as the calm water foams and boils around them.

The longest of the Medway tributaries, the River Beult joins the Medway just west of Yalding among the low-lying meadows of The Lees. This makes a pleasant green triangle between the confluence of the Beult and the Medway.

In summer, the Lees is fringed with cars, as people enjoy a picnic by the river, walk the dog or quench their thirst at the Anchor Inn, accessible by a footbridge across the canal. This old building might well have been there in Ireland's time. The garden spreads down to the water's edge, blooming with flowers, plastic tables and chairs, and drinkers of all ages. The air is thick with the smell of chips and beer. Now, the waterway bustles with motorboats and canoes laden with cargoes of holiday-makers in shorts and T-shirts, instead of freight-laden barges servicing towns along the Medway.

*A distant view of Yalding*

# Branbridges

*From Twyford bridge, the river bears its course eastward, through a fertile country whose meadows are famed for producing the largest, and best breed of cattle, in this county. The first picturesque object that presents itself deserving notice is Brantbridge, in the parish of East Peckham.*

Brandtbridge or Brandebrigge (Branbridges today) has been an important Medway crossing-place for many centuries, serving the route from London via Farningham and Wrotham Hill to all the Wealden country around Paddock Wood and beyond. At the time of Ireland's sketch, the Navigation Company was in full operation and the river would have been busy with commercial traffic. Branbridges was in the administrative district, or lathe, of Aylesford.

Ireland praises the *retired and romantic situation of this spot . . . one of those simple and interesting scenes, from the study of which Dutch and Flemish artists, as well as the judicious of our own country, have established a lasting fame.*

He would not have been so fulsome in his praise today for, in 1906, his medieval bridge was replaced by a sturdy utilitarian structure, recently rebuilt with steel beams, a reinforced concrete deck and parapets in Kentish ragstone. This early 20th century edifice, so different from the attractive curved bridge in Ireland's sketch, has been considered *unworthy of the pen* by our late 20th century artist. The road over the bridge is unremarkable, taking the motorist through an industrial estate and business park at East Peckham. A few hundred yards downstream, a further blot on this lovely stretch of the Medway is the railway bridge carrying the line from Maidstone to Paddock Wood. In 1998, Hale Street bypass was built with a further bridge across the river, leaving East Peckham in relative peace: *The various meanderings and recesses of the river affording perpetual scenes of that simplicity in nature, which produces the elegant in landscape.*

Ireland's words are still true along the stretch between Twyford and Tonbridge. Here the river twists and turns, widens and narrows, reflecting the thickly foliaged banks, overhanging trees and bright clumps of summer flowers. Below these green banks, sun, sky, trees and flowers are reflected on the river's glassy back in a chiaroscuro of mood.

Ireland mentions the many rivulets which cross the adjoining meadows, the most important of these being a branch of the River Teise which joins the Medway immediately above Twyford Bridge.

At Hartlake Bridge, Ireland was fascinated by the Flowing Bolt, *an ingineous contrivance to pen up the water to a certain degree, so that it may, in dry season . . . let out water to the neighbouring meadows.*

The Medway had only been made navigable here since 1740, and it is likely that Ireland had not seen anything similar before. Today, there are three locks between Twyford Bridge and Town Lock at Tonbridge. The reinforced concrete bridge at Hartlake, built in 1910, is a utilitarian structure in geometric steel, no doubt replacing a wooden bridge. Ireland comments on the trees along the border of the river and the *rich gardens of hops that are frequently intervening.*

Along the towpath upstream of Twyford, the *liquid serpent* meanders across eight-and-a-half miles of a wide, clay valley interspersed by locks. A few farms and oast-houses dot the fields of hops and rape, brooks and small tributaries swell the Medway, and the North Downs rise in the distance like a small wave; a gravel pit sits on the south bank like a giant pile of brown sugar. Although there are fewer hops, the overall scene cannot have changed much in 200 years.

The path on the north side of the river is a designated footpath called the Medway Valley Walk and takes the pedestrian into Tonbridge through a flat and fertile landscape. This attractive path is also part of the Weald Way which runs from Beachy Head in Sussex to Gravesend in Kent and passes through the castle grounds at Tonbridge. Upstream from Hartlake, the only sounds are birdsong, the low roar from the weirs, and the vibrating diesel engines of motor-cruisers slapping the banks with their echoing wash. These fibreglass pleasure-boats have replaced the working barges of Ireland's time. Today, it is the tourist not the tonnage of burthen that counts.

As Tonbridge nears, the roar of traffic from Canon Bridge is audible, and soon the gasometer and metal sheds of the industrial estate come into view. Crossing Vale Road through a continuous flow of cars, the pedestrian rejoins the towpath to Town Lock where the deserted Whitefriars Press, with its peeling weatherboards, is a reminder of the importance of the printing industry in Tonbridge.

# Tonbridge

*The principal stone bridge over the river at Tunbridge was begun in August 1775 . . . at a county expense of eleven hundred pounds . . . it is neat and substantial, calculated more for utility than ornament.*

The present Town bridge at Tonbridge was built in 1814, to carry the High Street over the Medway. In 1889, cast-iron beams replaced the arches, and in the 1920s it was widened. Today, every inch of its fifty-five feet is smothered in cars and lorries, fuming slowly along the congested High Street. The bridge has delicate, white, cast-iron railings, and the street lamps are crowned with hanging baskets, a splash of embroidered colour above a span of lace. Beyond the bridge, the ruins of the old castle rise from the trees as they did in Ireland's day. A diminishing group of Tudor houses cluster under the castle hill. From this historic centre, the modern town fans out to the north and the south like the loops of a large bow tie.

The motte-and-bailey castle at Tonbridge has had a stormy history. Ireland's *venerable ruins* are an enduring memorial to the Norman Conquest, for the castle was given to Richard Fitz Gilbert (known as Richard de Clare) for loyal services to William the Conqueror, as a reward for leaving his own castle of Brionne and following his king to England. He was also given considerable lands with which to support the upkeep of the castle, known as the 'lowy' of Tonbridge, and these included Halling, Barming, Aylesford, Cooling, and Leybourne, amongst others. The pragmatic Richard, determined not to be short-changed, had measured the perimeter of his lands at Brionne with a rope.

When William Rufus came to the throne, Ireland tells us that Odo, the *insatiable prelate, obtained the manor, with twenty-two others, from the See of Canterbury, in a way that did no great credit to his reputation.* Richard de Clare like Odo, dissatisfied with the new king, joined the *insatiable prelate* in a barons' revolt against William Rufus. This so infuriated the king that he sent a force against Tonbridge Castle which was captured in two days, and the timber castle and small town were burnt to the ground. After stirring up trouble in both Rochester and Tonbridge, Odo returned to his native Normandy, and in 1088 Richard de Clare retired to a monastery where he died three years later. However, Richard de Clare's descendants prospered, accumulating power, wealth, status, and eventually the titles, Earl of Hertford and Earl of Gloucester.

Moving rapidly through history, Edward, Duke of Buckingham, was the last of the warrior nobles to hold Tonbridge Castle, and was beheaded by Henry VIII for high treason. His estates were confiscated in 1520 and were surveyed and valued for the Crown. The report observed that 300 years after the peak of its glory, the gatehouse was still largely unrivalled in England. By the time Ireland was making his sketch, the castle had fallen into a bad state of repair:

*This famous castle, once the favoured seat of the first Peers and most exalted minds, affords at present little more than a subject for reflection on the vicissitudes of earthly greatness: its keep, which still remains, is overgrown with ivy, and its extensive walls . . . are now with as much caution preserved to bar the entrance of a curious and inquisitive traveller.*

Samuel Ireland Esq. was disappointed because he was not allowed access, and airs his views on the subject:

*Domestic privacy is unquestionably sacred . . . but in the commerce of the world some sacrifices have ever been made to public opinion and public curiosity; and at stated periods and prescribed seasons . . . the curtesy of the highest ranks of this kingdom has thrown open their gardens and palaces to the eye of the stranger and traveller.*

He would no doubt have approved of The National Trust and English Heritage, and been amused to see the castle swarming with inquisitive men, women and children today.

A gentleman called John Hooker became the new owner in 1739 and was soon using the castle as a quarry, selling off the old stone. He was a promoter of the Medway Navigation Company, and story has it that he used some of the castle's masonry to build locks on the river. His son, Thomas, plundered the ruins to build a small mansion to the east side of the gatehouse, which later became the offices of the Tonbridge District Council. In 1792, the castle was sold to William Woodgate who must have been the owner, so keen on his *'domestic privacy'*, that Ireland complains about. After this, under the direction of the trustees, the castle was used as a private home, a military academy in the 1860s, and finally as a boys' preparatory school. In 1897, the trustees sold the castle to Tonbridge District Council and the gatehouse, buildings and fourteen acres of land now belong to the people of Tonbridge.

At the close of the 20th century, the imposing sandstone 13th century gatehouse remains intact. The great archway and two massive roundels glow warmly in the peaceful sunshine, like the trunks of two immense stone trees. Held by the de Clares and Staffords, seized by Henry VIII, and fortified by Parliament, this gatehouse has defied 900 years of siege, insurrection, plunder and neglect.

Today, part of the 18th century addition is used as a tourist office, where visitors may purchase tickets to The Exhibition and Museum, opened in 1992, and sample a taste of the medieval experience. Armed only with a tape-recorder, the *curious and inquisitive traveller* can recapture the castle's heyday. Inside the gloomy gatehouse, the storerooms and guardrooms are lit only by flickering electric candles. Here, audio-visual displays and life-sized models take the visitor back to the 13th century. Climbing the steep stairs up to the roof of the tower, the visitor finds a dummy soldier in chain-mail on watch.

The panorama from this height shows the strategic importance of Tonbridge Castle, and why it was slighted in the 17th century so that it could no longer pose a threat. Below the hill, the steep, tiled roofs of the old houses have changed little. On the south side, the tall chimneys of the Jacobean house at Somerhill can be seen in the distance. Owned in the 18th century by the Earl of St Albans, it is now a preparatory school for boys and girls. An Iron Age camp can be seen on Castle Hill, but the old Priory between the Great Bridge and St Stephen's Church has long since disappeared.

If Samuel Ireland had been able to enjoy the same view today, he would not have recognised the huge gasometer near the river, the glass and concrete rectangles of West Kent College, nor the rows of brick houses marching up Quarry Hill. The Greensand Ridge rises to the north-east, while below, the 1864 stone buildings of Tonbridge School stand beside the manicured 1st XI cricket ground, known confusingly as The Head. The bright tiles of the 'pepper-pot' roof of the Old Big School are clearly visible, and the Kentish ragstone of the 14th century parish church and the 16th century Rose and Crown Hotel blends happily with the older buildings.

*Tonbridge School from near the Medway*

The castle grounds are now open to the public. The moat is a water-garden and wooden benches, placed conveniently on the lawns of the inner bailey, enable *the curious traveller* to enjoy a moment's peace, while looking down onto the quiet river and bustling High Street. Along the Riverside Walk, rowing boats for hire sit on the glassy water below the ancient moat, and visitors of all ages pass through the castle's well-kept grounds. Children's voices, quacking ducks and the low roar of traffic have replaced the sounds of clashing swords, horses hooves, and musket fire.

Tonbridge, according to Samuel Ireland, derived its name from the town of bridges. On this important route from London to the Channel ports there has been a crossing since Saxon times or even earlier. In the 17th century, Tonbridge became a market for the cloth and iron industries. At the same time, the naval dockyards increased their demand for timber and ordnance from the Weald, which prompted schemes to extend the navigation. Two years after Charles Stuart was restored to the throne, a bill was presented to Parliament for making the Medway navigable in the counties of

Kent and Sussex. This made sense, as transportation of iron ordnance, cannon balls, timber and other materials for His Majesty's Service would be easier on water than on land, where roads would have been impassable for much of the year. In addition, cargoes of timber, corn, hops, wool, leather, etc. could be sent down river, while coals, lime and stone would be shipped upstream. The bill became an act in 1664, but nothing was done for a further eighty years. Meanwhile, transport was improved by the introduction of the turnpike system, and a good stagecoach service passed through Tonbridge until superseded by the railway in the 1840s.

In 1740, powers were granted to make the Medway navigable from Forest Row in Sussex to *Mistress Edmond's Wharf in the town of Maidstone*. Ireland tells us that the Tonbridge Company took control of the locks, *all merchandize, except stone, pays four-pence per mile.* He adds that the statute does not seem to have been enforced with much effect *as it is now, in dry seasons, frequently not navigable.*

When The Company of Proprietors of the Navigation of the River Medway came into being, locks were built, essential work done to the banks and river bed, and a towpath laid down. By 1743, the company had its own fleet of barges, which turned Tonbridge from a sleepy market-town to a bustling commercial centre. This new navigation changed the face of the town. With bricks and mortar easily available, the old wooden buildings of Ireland's sketch were replaced by Georgian-style domestic and civic architecture. The Great Bridge, which had spanned the Medway here from medieval times, became a serious obstruction to boat traffic, as the locks had raised the water-level of the river. The old bridge was therefore demolished to the foundations, and the 1775 bridge, depicted by Ireland, took its place.

The Medway Company had a troubled future. Bad management, underfunding and litigation disputes took their toll, and the passing of the South Eastern Railway Company Act in 1836 dealt the death blow. The new railway ran from Redhill to Tonbridge and on to the coast and, in 1910, the company came into the hands of a receiver. However, a new company was formed and promoted a bill which resulted in the creation of the Medway Conservators. The whole navigation was remodelled and, by September 1915, the river was reopened at a cost of £90,000. After the First World War, further legislation brought into being the River Medway Catchment Board, superseded by the Kent River Board, the National Rivers Authority and now the Environment Agency.

Pollution is nothing new. In 1870, a critic wrote:

We cannot doubt that the place called the Locks is very fit for bathing . . . but, when barges go down the river they always bring down the tar with them and it is not pleasant to find oneself covered with tar . . . the water is not nearly so clear as it is above the town.

An anonymous ditty describes the water of the Medway in the bad old days: 'Truly, I receive some sewage, / Truly, I'm the drain of Tonbridge.'

In 1993, a Mission Statement from the Environment Agency boasts: 'We will protect and improve the water environment by the effective management of water resources and by substantial reduction in pollution. We will aim to provide effective defence for people and property against flooding from rivers and the sea. In discharging our duties we will operate openly and balance the interests of all who benefit from and use rivers, groundwaters, estuaries, and coastal waters.'

It is good to know that today it is only their duty that is being discharged, although the Environment Agency admits that 'low summer flows and high temperatures make Wealden rivers vulnerable to pollution, particularly from agricultural wastes'. In addition, the growth in population in commuter centres 'has resulted in treated effluent forming a high proportion of the base flow of rivers in the catchment area . . . Urban and industrial developments have also been significant in relation to the upper estuary, the principal discharges being treated effluents from the paper and chemical industries and sewage effluent from Aylesford and Snodland.'

Flooding has long been a problem throughout the Medway catchment area, where many towns have been developed in the flood plain. On 15 September 1968, spring tides and twenty-four hours of continuous rain produced the worst floods in living memory, affecting many of the villages west of Tonbridge, including Hever and Penshurst.

One housing estate, built in 1964-5, overlooked fields behind Hilden Manor which often flooded. Purchasers were assured that the new houses were eighteen inches above the highest recorded flood level. They were safe. However, that day, suburban security was shattered. Between 10 a.m. and 12 noon, without warning, the stream beside the estate burst its banks and eighteen inches of uninvited water poured through the front doors of the lower houses and bungalows. Residents were forced to forget Sunday lunch, pull on their wellingtons and evacuate. One young family's attempts were thwarted when their car stalled in the flooded River Eden near Leigh. A passing milk-float came to the rescue, and the driver pacified the screaming baby and wailing cat with a welcome 'pinta'. The family returned home and were taken in by neighbours on higher ground. In the afternoon, the waters abated and the owners returned to dry out their sodden bungalow, but that night the tide rose again and water, this time from the fields, poured stealthily in through the back doors, flooding the estate for a second time. As dawn broke, dazed sheep, rescued from the flooded fields, could be seen heading for London up the A21, leaving a trail of water behind them.

Tonbridge is now protected by a flood relief barrier, which lies in Haysden Park, one-and-a-half miles west of Tonbridge. The barrage was built in 1979-80 and is just one of the ways that the landscape around the Medway has been changed by the influence of transport developments, river management and gravel-pits.

The Haysden Country Park covers an area of 165 acres, occupying former pasture-land, and shows how successive engineering influences have shaped the local topography and land use. From the car park off Lower Haysden Lane, a well-signed path leads under the railway bridge to Barden Lake, once a gravel-pit and now used for dinghy sailing. Trees soften the lake side, and the bright foliage of willows spotlights an isolated island. Beside the sailing-club building, a green embankment rises to a maximum height of 5.7 metres, a latter-day Offa's Dyke, wrapping a defensive arm around the flood plain to defend Tonbridge from the Medway's wrath. The A21 viaduct, with its concrete 'tombstones', supports the great weight of this dual carriageway across the watery valley, cutting the rural landscape into two roaring halves.

The railway line from London Bridge to Dover, via Redhill, was opened in 1842 and crosses the Flood Relief Barrier on its own embankment. The future of this cross-country connection between Redhill and Tonbridge may be dramatically changed by the advent of the Channel Tunnel high-speed rail link.

The remnants of 19th century industrial enterprises are still visible. The Stone Lock was built in 1829 by James Christie in an attempt to challenge the monopoly of the Medway Navigation Company. He planned to extract valuable timber at Penshurst and carry it downstream in barges. The entrepreneurial Mr Christie even planned to extend the canal to Forest Row, Sussex, thence to the River Arun and finally to Portsmouth. Today, this weed-choked lock moulders away beside the busy railway, while the New Medway Channel carries the main flow of water from the control gates in the flood relief barrier. Meanwhile, the errant Medway, meanders feebly across the Shallows, more reeds than water, enjoyed only by the ducks. Through dank vegetation, the cylindrical mouths of Victorian brick culverts still gape above the sluggish water, eerie 19th century relics.

Natural disasters have also played a part in changing the landscape. On 16 October 1987, the Medway, Eden and Darent rivers were unusually high, and floodwaters lapped the fields. Between 2 a.m. and 6 a.m., hurricane-force winds tore at town and landscape, lifting off roofs, toppling church spires, and felling acres of mature trees. A memorial to this terrible night is an area of newly-planted trees called the Heusenstamm Friendship Wood near the control barrage. A series of pillboxes or mini forts, built along the banks of the Medway in case of invasion by the Germans, are still visible, now softened by blackthorn and brambles. It is ironic that it was Tonbridge's twin town of Heusenstamm in Germany, that donated trees and money to re-establish woodland after the great storm. These unlovely pillboxes have been left as part of Britain's military heritage, and a constant reminder of the threat of possible invasion.

Fish have returned to the Medway in recent years. The headwaters and tributaries support a small population of native brown trout and, in the deeper waters of the middle reaches, carp, gudgeon and tench are found. All these fish are mentioned by Ireland. In his day, salmon, trout and oysters were also commonplace, but now the poor quality of the industrialised estuary means these fish are rarely seen.

Today, the still waters of the Tonbridge Medway, downstream of the bridge, reflect 19th and 20th century brick buildings. On the north bank, the cupola-towered former National Westminster Bank is now a Pizza Express; in Ireland's sketch this was the building belonging to the Wise family, wood turners who manufactured the original Tunbridge Ware. The new office blocks opposite are a pastiche of the old warehouses. The Castle Inn, on the south side of the bridge, was built in 1760 as a hostelry, just when the town was beginning to expand. A plaque on the wall tells the passer-by the story of one of the inn's most famous customers, Knuckle Champion, Tom Sayers. Leaning on the bar, glass in hand, a week after his 42-round fight with John C.

Heenan, Sayers was heard to say, ' any man that licks me will have to kill me first.' It was to be his last fight.

Tonbridge, is a busy market-town with an important main line station where thousands of commuters, bristling with briefcases, lap-top computers, mobile phones and newspapers, cram themselves into railway carriages and rattle up to London in forty minutes. Every hour, the silver and gold Eurostar flashes through the station on its three-hour journey from Waterloo to Paris, while the ordinary commuter trains wait respectfully for their high-tech. relative to pass.

The town's famous boys' school, was a legacy from Richard de Clare, who founded a priory in his *manor of Tunbridge* in 1192. By the middle of the 14th century, the monastery was flourishing and, although burnt down in a disastrous fire, it was rebuilt, helped by the Archbishop of Canterbury who granted indulgence of forty days to all who helped to rebuild the priory. However, in 1525, Cardinal Wolsey decided to suppress the monasteries at Tonbridge and Bayham, and the priory was dissolved. To placate the indignant townspeople, Wolsey promised to found a local grammar school with exhibitions for forty scholars to attend his Oxford college. The plan was never implemented, as Wolsey fell from favour, and Tonbridge was left for thirty years without its priory or the promised school.

In 1553, an enlightened Tonbridge merchant called Andrew Judd, a Lord Mayor of London and Master of the Skinners' Company, came to the rescue. He obtained a charter to establish a *free grammar school* at Tonbridge and, to provide a suitable endowment, he purchased houses and land in the City and round St Pancras. It is due to the enhanced value of these lands that the school was able to expand and, at the present time, it is still governed by the Skinner's Company in accordance with Andrew Judd's wishes. In 1838, the then headmaster, Thomas Knox, levelled the cricket ground using earth and labour from the new railway workings, and the famous 1st XI ground became one of the two flattest pitches in the south of England. Since then, Tonbridge School has been synonymous with cricket. C.T. Dodd, a drawing master at the school from 1834-78, painted a well-known oil entitled *The Cricket Match at Tonbridge School, 1851.*

St Augustine's Chapel, built for Tonbridge School in the first few years of the 20th century, was destroyed by fire in 1988. Only the exterior fabric and most of the wall structure remained. This controversial Gothic-revival edifice had become a repository

Plate XXI

High Rocks

Plate XXII

Penshurst Place

Now, Penshurst, they that will proportion thee
With other edifices, when they see
Those proud, ambitious heaps, and nothing else,
May say, their lords have built, but thy lord dwells.

Ben Jonson

Plate XXIII

Bayham Abbey

of many mens' dreams and memories during the eighty-six years of its existence. In 1995, the remains of the original chapel were heavily restored, using similar materials. This restoration work was one of the largest ecclesiastical building projects undertaken in the country in recent years. The light marble and oak interior is brightened by soaring gold panels and three great brass candelabra, suspended from the lofty roof. A feeling of expectant space emanates from this elegant simplicity. Dedicated by the Bishop of Rochester on 20 October 1995, its regular use for services and concerts, attended by many visitors, would no doubt have met with Mr Ireland's approval.

*Among other objects most conspicuous within our view, is Somerhill, the residence of William Woodgate Esq. This venerable mansion was built by the Earl of St Albans, in the reign of Charles I.*

This grand Jacobean house, built in mellow sandstone, stands on a hill looking down at woods and fields towards the encroaching suburbs of south Tonbridge. With its gabled, tiled roofs, mullioned windows and clusters of chimneys, it stands proudly in its broad acres, like a well-preserved aristocrat amongst the espalier trees, cedars and clipped yew hedges.

The land was originally part of the Manor of South Frith and was presented by Elizabeth I to the only child of her minister, Sir Francis Walsingham. Ireland tells us a little about his daughter, Frances:

*. . . a lady the splendor of whose matrimonial connections, if we take into our consideration the rank and distinguished eminence of the persons chosen, has hardly been equalled in the history of female life.*

Her three husbands were certainly household names. The first, the soldier poet Sir Philip Sidney, died bravely in battle. The second, the ill-fated Earl of Essex, paid for his popularity with Queen Elizabeth I, and was executed on Tower Hill in 1601 after an unsuccessful military expedition. Her third husband was Richard Burgh, Earl Clanrickard, and together they built the present mansion early in the reign of James I.

Their son, Ulick, championed the Royalist cause and was forced into exile when his estate was sequestered by Parliament in 1645. The estate was then voted to John Bradshaw who had presided over the court which condemned Charles to death. Ireland calls Bradshaw a bloodhound, and philosophises: *This distinguised mansion affords us also another lesson of the instability of everything human.*

Ireland leaves the story here and moves swiftly on to Penshurst Place. However, the continuing history shows that, like kingdoms, great estates also rise and fall.

With the restoration of Charles II, the estate once more returned to its rightful owner, Ulick's only daughter, *the extraordinary lady Margaret Viscountess Purbeck*.

Meanwhile, Somerhill came into the possession of the Woodgate family and, at this time, Turner made a painting of the house which now hangs in the National Gallery of Scotland. With the advent of the agricultural depression during the Napoleonic Wars, the Woodgate family fell on hard times; the estate went on the market and was sold to James Alexander in 1816. The victorious Duke of Wellington declined to purchase Somerhill, as he was dissatisfied with the fox-hunting there. In 1849, Sir Isaac Lyon Goldsmid bought the house, and the D'Avigdor Goldsmid family remained there until 1980. Sir Isaac's grandson, Julian, had eight daughters in his attempt to produce a male heir, so the house nearly doubled in size. Julian's wife must have had something to do with this labour of love.

Today, Lady D'Avigdor Goldsmid, once lady-in-waiting to the second Queen Elizabeth, lives at the Old Laundry in Tudeley. Tragically, the family lost their daughter, Sarah, in a sailing accident in 1963 and, as a memorial to her life, the artist Marc Chagall designed a radiant set of windows in Tudeley Church.

In 1988, the house and estate were acquired as a new home for Yardley Court School, a preparatory school for boys, joined in 1993 by Derwent Lodge for girls. There is also a mixed pre-preparatory school for children from three to seven years. These fortunate children are carefully nurtured under the exquisite stucco ceilings of a stately home which still overlooks a small patch of unspoiled Kent.

# Penshurst Place

*Penshurst Place, if we alone take into our consideration the celebrity of its former possessor, the gallant and all-accomplished Sir Philip Sydney, could not properly have been passed unnoticed; but it has in itself, as a spacious and venerable remain of antiquity, a still higher claim to our attention.*

Of all Ireland's *venerable* buildings, Penshurst is his most *venerable and extensive pile.* He writes pages of history, eulogises the accomplishments and character of the great soldier-poet, Sir Philip Sidney, and quotes verses from 17th century bards when he runs out of superlatives. Interestingly, he comments on the decayed and neglected state of the building . . . *it is with regret I contemplate the probability of a total decay of this mansion of Heroes. Should that event take place, and no stone remain to indicate its former greatness, yet shall imagination fondly trace the spot where Sydney first drew breath . . .*

In spite of Ireland's concern, it can be seen from his sketch that Penshurst Place was in better condition than many of his chosen subjects. It is the great size of this heroic mansion which poses a problem for him:

*It is to be regretted, that the size of this undertaking is rather too confined to admit of an illustration of all the parts of this noble and extensive building.* With a rare apology for artistic licence, he manages to obtain *the best point of view for comprizing the whole, in which the church of Penshurst . . . is included.*

Penshurst Place and gardens invite superlatives. The great house we see today has developed from a 14th century manor house, fortified by the wealthy merchant Sir John de Pultney who built the barons' hall, one of the grandest in the country. Over the centuries, generations of distinguished owners have enlarged this lavish house, using local sandstone, brick and timber, in a sympathetic amalgam of architectural styles.

In 1552, Edward VI made a special gift of Penshurst Place and its 4,000 acre estate to Sir William Sidney of Flodden Field renown, who was also Edward's tutor and steward from his birth until his coronation. The property has remained with the Sidney family ever since. Sir William's son, Henry, was Edward's childhood companion at court. Legend has it that the young king died in his arms. Sir Henry made a good marriage to Lady Mary Dudley, and became a trusted servant of Elizabeth I. He was given weighty responsibilities in Ireland for over twenty years and, in 1564, made a Knight of the Garter. For all this rank and honour, he was poorly rewarded and, by 1583, fell into debt, complaining that he had, 'not so much land as would graze a mutton.' However, this did not prevent him making substantial additions to the house, taking care to preserve its medieval character. The family coffers were replenished when his son, Sir Robert Sidney, Ist Earl of Leicester, inherited considerable riches from his uncles, Lady Mary Dudley's brothers, Robert Dudley, Earl of Leicester, and Ambrose, Earl of Warwick, who died without legitimate heirs.

Sir Henry's son, Philip Sidney, was born in 1554. Ireland lists his virtues enthusiastically . . . *he was wise and learned in the schools; gallant in the field; and, as a courtier, as free from the pedantry of the one, as from the boisterous manners of the other.*

Queen Elizabeth I would not let him be nominated for the Crown of Poland, . . . *lest she should lose "the jewel of her time"*. However, she reluctantly granted Philip permission to fight in Holland when the Dutch rebelled against Spain, and Sir Philip joined the Earl of Leicester, who was commanding the forces in the Low Countries as Governor of Flushing. In September 1586, he was mortally wounded on the battlefields of Zutphen. In a final act of chivalry, Philip gave the last of his water to another dying soldier with the immortal phrase, 'thy necessity is yet greater than mine'. Sir Philip Sidney died a month later, and was buried with due pomp and ceremony in St Paul's Cathedral.

Samuel Ireland must have the last word on this exceptional man:

*These extraordinary distinctions at home and abroad, the correctness of his morals, and the heroism and humanity which he displayed in the closing act of his life, place him as a scholar, a statesman, a soldier, and a man, in as elevated a point of view as human nature has ever been known to attain.*

By the 18th century, the fortunes of Penshurst Place were in decline. The 7th Earl of Leicester, Jocelyn, unlike his noble forebear, led an indecorous life, and sold the 2nd Earl's great library to pay for his pleasures. His only child was an illegitimate daughter, Anne, who married Henry Streatfeild of Chiddingstone Castle, and attempted to wrest the ownership of the house from her legitimate cousins. When

Jocelyn died, in 1743, the Leicester earldom died with him. William Perry inherited the property, spent money on modernising the estate, adding a plethora of fashionable sash windows and filled the building with a quantity of gilt furniture purchased on his grand tour. It took the family 200 years to remove these so-called 'improvements'. William Perry also produced six children and, while his family was still young, he was certified as a lunatic and died in an asylum in 1757. Only one of his children, Elizabeth Jane, married; her husband, Sir Bysshe Shelley, was grandfather of the famous poet Percy Bysshe Shelley. Percy was an admirer of his distant relative Sir Philip Sidney, held strong political,moral and religious convictions, and both men died unnaturally just before their thirty-second birthdays.

Penshurst Place was inherited by John Shelley-Sidney when he was only a boy. The estate, badly managed by the trustees, was in danger of falling into ruin. However, when John reached maturity, he took on an ambitious programme of restoration inside and out. In 1818, he was created Baronet of Penshurst, and the social revival of the family began.

Succeeding generations of Sidneys continued to lavish care and attention on the property and William, the 6th Lord De L'Isle and Dudley, had the daunting task of resurrecting the house after the damage and neglect of the Second World War. He was a remarkable man, one of only three men ever to have been awarded both of the highest orders of gallantry and chivalry - the Victoria Cross and the Knight of the Garter. In spite of shortages of food, money, fuel, and building materials in the postwar years, Penshurst Place was reopened to the public in 1947. Fifty years on, this *venerable and extensive pile* stands graciously in beautiful formal gardens, where herbaceous borders are walled in by clipped yew hedges. Eleven acres of gardens within gardens set off the mellow stones of this 600-year-old aristocrat which, in turn, is surrounded by a mantle of parkland and the rich green landscape of rural Kent.

The Sidney Oak, reputed to have been planted at the christening of Sir Philip Sidney in 1554, still stands in the grounds, a balding old man with a huge paunch. Two hundred years ago Ireland sketched the tree, noting that it measured twenty-two feet (6.7 metres) in circumference..*and within the hollow of its spacious trunk is affixed a seat capable of receiving several persons.* He was unable to resist the following verse by the 17th century poet, Edmund Waller:

Go, boy, and carve this passion on the bark

Of yonder tree, which stands the sacred mark

Of noble Sydney's birth; when such benign,

Such more than mortal-making stars did shine;

That there they cannot but for ever prove

The monument, and pledge of humble love.

The tree is in fact 1,000 years old. When it finally dies, it will have begat many more trees at home and abroad, for its acorns have been planted all round the park, and the 1st Viscount De L'Isle always carried a handful with him on his travels around the world. However, at the end of the 20th century, great oaks do not only grow from little acorns for, in its final years, this famous tree is to be cloned. In the process of micro-propagation, buds taken from the only remaining live branch will be sterilised and grown in a culture solution before being planted.

In 1991, Philip, the 2nd Viscount De L'Isle, inherited Penshurst Place and its estate. He has now made it his home with Isobel, his wife and their two children. Like their famous forebears, they will add their share to this *spacious and venerable remain of antiquity*, which is enjoyed by visitors of all ages and nationalities. A footpath, leading from the 13th century church, crosses the park where the green baize of the cricket field is backdropped by the mellow sandstone of the great house . From the rising ground to the east, Penshurst Place and Church stand gracefully among mature trees, which have been joined by younger trees, forming part of a ten year restoration scheme. On a summer's evening, when the air is filled with the scent of new-mown grass, and the only sounds are bleating sheep, the click of bat on ball, and peals of church bells, this is a scene that is 'forever England'.

At Penshurst, the Medway is joined by the Eden. This little river flows beneath high banks, cushioned with grasses and wild flowers, on its way to Chiddingstone and Hever.

*In the churchyard, Penshurst*

# Hever Castle

*The remain of the ancient castle of Hever, here presented, is nearly perfect in its exterior form.*

Samuel Ireland would have been pleased to see the transformation that this building has undergone this century, for today it is the perfect American dream of an English castle.

Ireland tells us that Hever Castle was built by William De Hever, in Edward III's reign. It came by marriage to the Cobham family *from whom it derived the name Hever Cobham,* before being sold to Anne Boleyn's grandfather. Anne's father, Sir Thomas Bullen, completely restored this castle in about 1500 adding a comfortable Tudor dwelling-house inside the protective wall. It was here that Henry VIII paid court to his ill-fated daughter, Anne. Ireland adds . . . *the apartment in which she slept, still retains her name. Several letters of the amorous tyrant are now existing, which are addressed to her at this place.*

There is no sign of Anne's name in her bedroom today, or the 'amorous tyrant's' letters, but Anne's two hand-illuminated Book of Hours (prayer books) are on view under glass. One has the poignant words *le temps viendra (the time will come)* written in her own hand, and in the other she has written, *remember me when you do pray / that hope doth lead from day to day.* She took this little book with her to her execution on Tower Hill on 19 May 1536. It is interesting to note that Henry VIII gave Anne Boleyn a beautiful gold clock as a wedding present, a replica of which can be seen in the Exhibition Room at Hever Castle. Time did not serve this young queen well.

After Sir Thomas's death, Henry seized the castle and land and granted them in 1541 to Lady Anne of Cleves . . . *whose fate,* (Ireland writes), *though short of death, was little less unfortunate. After her repudiation, this castle became her residence; and she held it on the hard terms of not being suffered to quit the realm without the King's consent.*

Current thinking assumes that Anne of Cleves settled happily in this country. As compensation for her divorce she was given precedence over all other ladies in England, except the queen and princesses, and received generous lifetime settlements which included Hever Castle. Having escaped from the *amorous tyrant,* and kept her head, her fate seems to us anything but unfortunate.

When Anne of Cleves died in 1557, the castle reverted to the Crown, and was given to Sir Edward Waldegrave by Queen Mary. For the next 160 years there followed a period of prosperity, and the family became the first baronets of Hever Castle when Sir Edward Waldegrave was granted the title in 1642. In 1745, it was purchased by Timothy Waldo Esq. in whose family, Ireland tells us, *it now remains.*

The longest freeholders of this period were the Meade-Waldos, owners from 1749 until 1903. During these years the castle went into serious decline, and became no more than a picturesque ruin, ideal for artists like Samuel Ireland to paint. However, in 1903, it was rescued by a wealthy American Europhile, William Waldorf Astor. This energetic millionaire, disenchanted with his own country, settled in England, purchasing Cliveden in Buckinghamshire, and Hever Castle. William Astor set about restoring the castle with all the comforts of the 20th century, while preserving its historic character. He resisted enlarging the castle and, instead, built the mock Tudor village to accommodate guests and staff, which entailed moving both the bed of the River Eden and the public road. These disparate but homogeneous buildings huddle deferentially behind the castle, much as an older village might have done in medieval days.

During their eight decades at Hever, the Astor family distinguished themselves in every field of endeavour. In 1963, Gavin, 2nd Baron Astor of Hever, decided to open the castle and grounds to the public for the first time. The gardens had been laid out on their present grand scale between 1904 and 1908. It took over 1,000 men to create the classical Italian garden, dig the thirty-five acre lake and transport Scots pines from Ashdown Forest.

At the end of the 20th century, the gardens have reached full maturity and are enjoyed by thousands of visitors of all nationalities. The compact little castle, with moat and drawbridge intact, stands in gardens where formality blends with informality in an undulating landscape of mature trees, flowering shrubs and colourful herbaceous borders. Topiary yews and herb gardens blend with orchards; rhododendrons and azaleas pour colour down the slopes and along walkways; and the blooms of a walled rose-garden blaze throughout the summer months. The sophisticated Italian garden is filled with classical sculptures, the statues mainly collected by William Astor while he was American Minister in Rome. The great loggia at the lake side is a triumphant edifice which would certainly have met with Mr Ireland's approval. Flanked with colonnades, it descends by balustraded steps to the piazza below, where a magnificent fountain supported by two female figures is carved in Pentelic marble, a deluge of classical elegance set in the natural beauty of the Kent countryside.

Inside and out, the castle, pristine as a freshly wrapped gift, is lavishly furnished with imported antiques and paintings. The panelled rooms, a riot of intricate carvings carefully matched with 16th and 17th century furniture, are small enough to feel warm and intimate, a home as well as a castle, so different from the disintegrating remains sketched by Ireland in 1793.

In 1981, the Astor family and their trustees decided to sell Hever Castle and its surrounding estate of about 3,500 acres. The whole estate was bought in 1983 by Broadland Properties Limited, a Yorkshire-based private company. Today, concerts and plays are held on the loggia, and the pavilion is used for teas and income-generating functions. Visitors may walk and picnic in the grounds and enjoy, at leisure, one of England's great gardens.

Ireland is dismissive of Hever village: *The neighbouring village of Hever has little to recommend it to notice.* There is only a brief mention of the altar-tomb in the church, erected to the memory of the Earl of Wiltshire, father to Anne Boleyn. Ireland then turns his attention to nature, telling his reader: *the neighbourhood is famed for its fertile production of oak trees, which grow to an uncommon large size.*

Apart from the church, pub and a few cottages, there is little else to the village today. The church is beautifully tended, smelling of lilies and new-mown grass. The famous monumental brass of Sir Thomas Bullen is one of the finest in the country, and still lies on the impressive tomb in the Bullen Chapel. It was in danger of being elbow-greased away by brass-rubbing enthusiasts, but a facsimile is now available, and Sir Thomas can rest in peace. The oldest tomb in the church is that of John de Cobham, who took possession of Hever Castle in 1380 and died in 1399.

The view from Hever car park looks north across acres of unspoiled rolling countryside, dotted with oak trees and oast-houses. The scene would be reassuringly familiar to Samuel Ireland, unlike the stream of circling jets preparing to land at Gatwick airport.

Returning to the Medway at Penshurst, Ireland comments: *As this part of the river affords no object particularly attractive, I shall pursue its eastern direction towards Tunbridge Wells.*

The Medway from Penshurst to Tunbridge Wells flows through some beautiful, unspoiled countryside but is certainly devoid of *venerable buildings*. In the 18th century, unspoiled countryside was a plentiful commodity, and therefore not the attraction that it is today.

A smaller river now, the Medway snakes furtively beneath high banks, where thistles, ragged robin, and meadow-sweet sway above the reeds and nettles. Orange, blue and yellow butterflies flit across the towpath, rising and falling, in evanescent flight. Greens and browns paint a still-life in the reflecting water, where the electric blue threads of damselflies, hover like diaphanous chromosomes. Now and then, the river comes to life: frothing busily over stones or disused weirs, then carves its way once more between banks, green-fringed with oak, ash and willow. Only the tapping of woodpeckers and the clatter of startled pigeons disturb the silence. Swifts and martins swoop low for insects across the brown water, where jumping fish ring the stillness.

Pylons, iron aliens, stride across the fields among the ruminating cows and sheep. Here and there, the white cowl of an oast-house peeps through clumps of trees. Along this stretch, the Medway flows through the meadows, in a landscape that has changed little in 200 years, *fertilizing this celebrated county . . . the beautiful meandering of its course affords that perpetual diversity of objects which cannot fail to attract and yield gratification to the admirers of rural scenery.*

The village of Ashurst (Wood of Ashes, presumably from the iron-smelting of the Weald) is mentioned in connection with a wooden crucifix:

*Ashurst, . . . once famed for the superstition of its inhabitants, whose credulity was so great, as to believe in the growth of the nails and hair, and even of the body, of a wooden crucifix, which was occasionally shewn to them by their wily priest . . . himself probably grew sleek and fat, upon this addition to his benefice.*

It is possible that this *wily priest* knew of the *miraculous* dynamic crucifix at Boxley Abbey.

*Between this village and Groombridge the Medway again takes several directions towards Ashdown and Waterdown Forests, in Sussex, where it is supplied by various springs.*

# Groombridge Place

*Groombridge . . . is within the parish of Speldhurst; it has formerly been a place of much note, and was anciently called Gromenebregge, a name probably derived from that of a noble Saxon, who is reputed to have been its original proprietor, and from whom it came to the family of the Cobhams and the Clintons: they sold it to the renowned Knight, Sir Richard Waller, who accompanied Henry V into France, and there highly distinguished himself in the field of Agincourt.*

Groombridge Place, originally a moated stronghold, lies on the borders of Kent and Sussex and would have been of strategic importance. The River Grom, no more than a stream, flows along a lush valley from High Rocks, and joins the Medway at Hamm Farm between Groombridge and Withyham.

Groombridge was the property of the Waller family from 1360 to 1604. Sir Richard Waller, grandson of the purchaser, fought gallantly at Agincourt and Ireland tells the traditional story:

*In that famous battle he is said to have found the Duke of Orleans amidst the slain, with small signs of life remaining, when, by the King's order, he was committed to the care and custody of this Knight, who conducted him prisoner to Groombridge. At this mansion he was kept in honourable confinement twenty-five years. On paying four hundred thousand crowns for his ransom he obtained his release; and so highly was he satisfied with the liberal treatement of his generous host, that he rebuilt his mansion and repaired the parish church over which his arms are still to be seen.*

As a further mark of gratitude, this illustrious prisoner, Ireland tells us, assigned to Sir Richard and his heirs for ever, the escutcheon of France, suspended on a walnut-tree, with the motto, '*Hi fructus virtutis*' (This is the fruit of valour). Whether this legend is true or false, the fleur-de-lys is undeniably incorporated into the Waller coat of arms, which can be seen in the oldest stained glass window in the church.

Accounts of Ireland's anecdote vary, but it seems that the French prisoner was the Duke of Orleans's younger brother, Jean of Angouleme, taken hostage aged twelve, three years before the Battle of Agincourt. He spent some time in custody at Groombridge, returning to France in 1442. Meanwhile, his famous brother, Charles, was a prisoner in Starborough Castle, just over the Surrey border.

Robert H. Goodsall, in his book on the Medway, tells us that the myth was perpetuated when a tablet inscription was put up in the Church of St John in 1826. The inscription: *Sir Richard Waller of Groombridge by whom Charles Duke of Orleans was rescued at the battle of Agincourt,* is clearly visible today on one of the south windows. St Johns' Church was built by John Packer in 1625, on the site of an older chapel, as a thank-offering for the safe return of Prince Charles from Spain in 1623, his coronation year. It was then a private chapel for Groombridge Place. Today it is a parish church, but the plume of feathers of King James I is carved over the porch with a Latin inscription to the effect that: *J.P. (John Packer) gave this shrine on account of the most fortunate return of Prince Charles from the Spaniards.* The inscription is dated 1625.

It is certain that the property passed to John Packer, Clerk to the Privy Seal during Charles I's reign, and the present house was built by Philip Packer in 1662. With the Civil War over, there was no need for an outer wall, but the moat was retained. The result is an Elizabethan H-plan, redbrick, moated manor-house with dormer windows under a hipped roof. Lying in a peaceful valley, sheltered by Groombridge Hill, this mellow, brick-and-tile mansion has changed little. Set amidst formal gardens with stone walls and clipped yews, it looks out onto unspoiled countryside. The warm trunks of redwood trees stand sentinel before the house, while Scots pines and mature hardwoods soften the undulating scene of woods and fields. Drifts of daffodils and wood anemones brighten the green banks of lake and river. The geometric moat is enjoyed by black and hooper swans, and crossed by delicately curved stone bridges.

Four generations of Packers owned the Manor from 1618-1734. The last male member of the Groombridge branch of the Packer family died in 1709, when the family's fortunes were already in decline and, by 1734, the estate became vested in Chancery. In 1754, William Camfield, a wealthy yeoman of the parish of Speldhurst, bought the estate and rescued it from its ruinous condition. The table-tombs of William and his family are grouped near the church porch.

At the end of the 18th century, Groombridge Place Estate belonged to Robert and Sarah Burges, and their initials can still be seen on the clock face of the church. The property then passed to The Reverend John James Saint, Rector of Speldhurst from 1839 - 1880; Miss Elizabeth Saint, the last surviving daughter, died in 1918. She and her sister, Miss Louisa, are reported to have had 'leanings to the supernatural' and were friendly with Sir Arthur Conan Doyle who lived in Crowborough and was a frequent visitor; he set his Sherlock Holmes story *Valley of Fear* at Groombridge Place. Sightings of the ghost of an ostler, who was drowned in the moat in 1808, have been reported, and story has it that this ostler asked Sir Arthur for a lift after he had dined at Groombridge Place. Nearing Crowborough, Sir Arthur turned round to ask his passenger where he wanted to alight. The back of the car was empty.

After the death of Miss Elizabeth Saint, Groombridge Place and the Estate were purchased by the Mountain family (founders of Eagle Star Insurance) and kept much as it had been in Packer's day. Their aim was to preserve the Place, Church and Old Village as a treasure for posterity.

The last occupant was Rosemary Newton, a niece of the Mountain family who died in 1991. Groombridge Place and the village were put up for auction in 1992, and the main house and parkland were purchased by the present owner, Andrew de Candole. The village was bought by The Bradford Property Trust and the farms by individuals.

Since 1992, imagination, time and money have been lavished on Groombridge Place Gardens. Around 70,000 visitors a year enjoy entering a world where make-believe becomes a reality. The 17th century formal gardens, laid out in their original grid-pattern, are less functional and more ornamental today, but retain a sense of peace and elegance in this English arcady. A giant chess set, oriental and secret gardens, and an enchanted forest, all portray a wonderland enjoyed by children of all ages. The ancient moat, millpond, river, streams and fountains enhance the feeling of tranquillity. Now, the bull-pen is a scented shop, the milking parlour a replica of Conan Doyle's study, milking sheds are tearooms, and the Baronial Hall is used for wedding ceremonies. Peacocks and birds of prey entertain the visitors, a thriving vineyard produces good wine, and acres of sunflowers brighten the fields in late summer. To the credit of Andrew de Candole and his planners, Groombridge Place faces the 21st century with confidence, retaining its traditional dignity despite this new-found commercialism.

Having recounted the legend of Groombridge's French prisoner, incorrectly thought to be the Duke of Orleans, Ireland leaves Groombridge and turns his attention to High Rocks. There is no sketch of Groombridge Place, and it would seem probable that this was one of the places he never visited at all.

*Groombridge Place*

# High Rocks and Tunbridge Wells

*Between Groombridge Place and the Wells, the immense craggy rocks and deep vallies . . . yield a more noble species of scenery than has yet presented itself in this pursuit . . . This romantic and retired scenery is within two miles of the Wells, and is a retreat much frequented by the company who resort thither.*

Like so many visitors, Ireland was fascinated by the *rocky prominences* which lie in and around Tunbridge Wells . . . *little doubt remains of their being the effect of some violent convulsion of the earth . . . but at what period this may have happened, philosophy is not able to trace, nor history reveal.*

The Weald itself has been formed over millions of years. The basic rocks became a lagoon, the size of south-east England, into which the deposits from several rivers laid down thick layers of sand, clays, stones and grit, in a series known today as Hastings beds. The *violent convulsion* produced a long domal anticline which creased into ridges and folds; Tunbridge Wells lies within the most northerly series of these folds. The massive sandstone ridge of Tunbridge Wells runs from Langton along Mount Ephraim and across the steep incline of London and Grosvenor Roads, and many of the town's finest buildings have been built from sandstone, quarried from this ridge. Toad Rock at Rusthall, Wellington Rocks on the Common, Penn's, Harrison's, Bowles' and High Rocks are the best known surviving outcrops, thrown out from the fault line of the sandstone ridge.

Samuel Ireland's sketch depicts a group of the High Rocks, and his information regarding these and Adam's Well is lifted straight from the earliest guide to Tunbridge Wells by Benge Burr in 1776, whose information was echoed in Sprange's guide ten years later. Using identical wording, Ireland writes:

*Some of these eminences are more than seventy feet in height, and strike the beholder from the vallies beneath, with a peculiar degree of pleasure and astonishment.*

Ireland, who may never have visited Tunbridge Wells, has nothing further to add on the subject. Sprange's 1786 guide describes the rocks as "stupendous ruins of nature" and tells us how impressed the Duke of York (later James II) was when he visited High Rocks with his family in 1670. A maze and a bowling-green with gambling facilities added spice to nature's ruins and, later, teas were served and fishing and boating permitted on the lake.

Today, the rocks are less astonishing to a population that has easy access to dramatic scenery elsewhere. However, they have attracted a steady stream of visitors since Ireland's time, arriving this century by car or train. Little has changed inside the turnstiles. Giant boulders are scattered or grouped in a pastoral setting; graded steps and wooden bridges take the intrepid visitor over the chasms, and the dramatic rocks make a perfect backdrop for photographs, especially of weddings. The High Rocks halt at one time had fourteen trains a day stopping for visitors to the rocks. It was closed in 1952, but the Eridge line was reopened in 1996, having been restored by volunteers. Now known as the Spa Valley Railway, steam trains once again take passengers from the former Tunbridge Wells West Station to Groombridge via High Rocks. The old station, built in 1866, is now a Beefeater Restaurant overlooking acres of parking area outside Sainsbury's superstore.

At the end of the 20th century it is the 19th century High Rocks Inn which attracts large numbers of visitors. Recently enlarged, its premises cater for smart functions where patrons can wine, dine and dance in sophisticated rustic barns. History lives on in names like The Halt and The Bell Room.

Ireland now mentions Adam's Well . . . *a limpid spring of very delicious water; the virtues of which seem to be of still more ancient date than the adjacent wells at Tunbridge.*

Ireland quotes the last verse of a poem in Sprange's guide: 'Yields to its balmy power; / Disabled limbs, inflamed eyes' / And bosome full of plaintive sighs, / Are soften'd ev'ry hour.' He adds, *this Well may fairly rival the waters of Lethe, for here all chronic and other complaints, not to except the pangs arising from the tender passion, may be removed.*

Such a panacea made healthy competition for the famous Chalybeate mineral spring on the Pantiles. Chalyps is Greek for iron, and it is this mineral which gives the water its distinctive taste and colour.

*Adam's Well near Langton Green*

Two-and-a-half miles from Tunbridge Wells, on the footpath to Groombridge, Adam's Well is the name on the gate of a smallholding. A Victorian cottage hugs the hill, overlooking an artificial lake enjoyed by a variety of fish and fowl. The *limpid spring* was probably once a Holy Well, which was purchased in 1765 by a Mr Pinchbeck whose horses, Ireland tells us, *had been materially benefitted by the use of the waters.* The entrepreneurial Mr Pinchbeck, a former master of a Tunbridge Wells Assembly Room, built a commodious stone bath here and declared these waters free for public use, in order, he declared, to induce more company to visit Tunbridge Wells and sell the water there and in London.

No doubt, too delicate a subject for Samuel Ireland's *Picturesque Views*, the fate of the well is recorded by Sprange: '. . . the vigilance of the managers was dropped, low company admitted . . . indecencies encouraged.' In short, it was no place for the fair sex, and a disgusted Tunbridge Wells left it to the weeds and brambles.

Although Rusthall, Tonbridge, Southborough and Mount Ephraim were all cashing in on the Pantiles popularity, offering lodging-houses and amenities, it was Mount Sion, conveniently near the precious Chalybeate spring, which won the day. Houses from the surrounding villages were transferred wholesale, often wheeled on platforms to be fixed on Mount Sion, 'this new seat of favour.' Burr describes up demise of the competition with humour:

> Thus in the course of a few years we find Tunbridge forsaken; Southborough and Rusthall raised and ruined; Mount Ephraim drooping; and Mount Sion in full bloom of prosperity.

Turning briefly to the medicinal waters at Tunbridge Wells, Ireland writes: *The efficacy of the medicinal waters at Tunbridge Wells are so well known as to render a minute history of them unnecessary.*

A short history of the town follows, lifted straight from Burr: *The springs then opened were seven in number, which were soon afterwards resorted to by mulitudes of the middling and lower class of people, who received great benefit from them.*

> *These springs, being on the borders of Lord Abergavenny's estates, it became his interest to give them every advantage in his power; he therefore cleared them of all incumbrances, ordered wells to be sunk, a pavement to be laid round them, and the whole to be enclosed with wooden rails.*

By the turn of the 17th century the 'spaw' habit became increasingly popular. Having been tried and tested by these lesser mortals, the springs were then visited in 1630 by Queen Henrietta Maria, wife of Charles I. She was ostensibly recovering from the birth of her son, the future king, Charles II, but no doubt was glad to escape from the rigours of court life and enjoy a sojourn in the country. As there was no suitable accommodation for visitors of any sort, let alone royalty, a camp was set up on Bishop's Down itself, with masques laid on for the young Queen's amusement. Ireland takes up the story:

*She is said to have one day walked from the well into the borders of Sussex, where, growing weary, she sat down on a bank for repose, after which she ordered a stone to be placed there in remembrance of her excursion; and some adulatory lines were added thereto by one of her attendants. Of the stone, or inscription, no trace is to be found; but the spot has served as a resting place for many a weary traveller since her time, as an ale house has been erected thereon, in the road to Frant, and is known by the sign of the Black Dog.*

There is no sign of a pub called the Black Dog today, and searches have not traced its whereabouts.

Ireland has already described Charles II as a *motley monarch* for his disastrous neglect of Medway defences which led to the Dutch invasion of 1667. Prejudices are well to the fore in the following excerpt:

*Tunbridge Wells, in the reign of Charles II, was much patronized by his Queen and the Royal Family, and under such dissipated influence it became as much the seat of gaiety and fashion, as the resort of disease and infirmity. About this period every improvement and accommodation took place; and it has since continued, particularly with the persons of the first fashion, to hold the highest rank amongst our places of public resort.*

The term 'merry monarch' might have been more appropriate, for the Merrie England of the Restoration wanted not only cures, but enjoyable diversions. It became the rallying point of the *fair and gallant of both sexes* and, in the words of Hamilton de Grammont, 'the place of all Europe the most rural and simple and yet, at the same time, the most entertaining and agreeable.' Drinking up to fifteen pints of the metallic brown liquid at dawn, to effect a cure, certainly needed some diversions.

A certain Dr Patrick Madan wrote in 1671 that the waters contained a calcauteous or vitriolic juice, which moved the belly to blackish secretion and provoked plentiful urine. As if this was not enough it also depauperated blood, blackening the drinker's tongue with sooty sulpherous minims, and producing nidorolent (sic) belches and eructations as if he had eaten hard fried eggs. However, with the physician's aid, it would dispel giddiness, passions of the heart, fainting of the spirits, hypochondriac and hysteric fits, and cure obstructions of the liver, spleen, scurvy and mad-dog bites. He added that Venus herself, 'rises Tryumphing in our hemisphere, at Tunbridge, generously imparting and distributing this impregnating Faculty to her Votaries, in order to preserve and perpetuate mankind.'

Katharine of Braganza, wife of Charles II, came in the hope that Venus would give her a son and heir. Although unsuccessful, the Stuarts continued to patronize Tunbridge Wells for the 'gynaecology of the place,' or perhaps for the scandal. Hamilton de Grammont clearly enjoyed all its attractions: 'the company, though always numerous, is always select: since those who go thither for diversions ever exceed the number of those who go thither for health, everything there breathes with pleasure; constraint is banished, familiarity established upon the first acquaintance, and joy and pleasure are the sole sovereigns of the place.'

Samuel Ireland describes one of the specialities of the Wells, which today would strike fury into the heart of all bird-lovers:

*the delicious wheat-ear, or English ortolan, should not be forgotten. These birds, during the summer season, are found in great abundance on the South Downs, where, to catch them the shepherds make little holes about a foot long and six inches broad, in which they place snares of horsehair; the birds, being fearful of rain, run into these holes for shelter, on the approach of every cloud, and are caught in great numbers.*

The consumption of vast quantities of Chalybeate spring water, together with the fresh air, described by Ireland as *peculiarly salubrious,* gave the company hearty appetites. Defoe, amongst others, hailed the wheatear as 'the most delicious taste for a Creature of one Mouthful as can be imagined'. In 1695, William Congreve, the dramatist, impressed by the quantity of food consumed, writes: 'You would not think how people eat here, everybody has the appetite of an ostrich, and, as they drink steel in the morning, so I believe at noon they could digest iron.'

Another luxury item is mentioned briefly by Ireland:

*The produce of the surrounding country is fertile in the growth of the holly, sycamore, yew and other trees from which an ingenious manufactory of useful and elegant inlaid works has been established.*

Samuel Ireland was referring to Tunbridge Ware, and tells us no more about it. The reader might assume that he was unfamiliar with these *elegant inlaid works* which were manufactured at the turn of the 17th century. The inlaid and mosaic wood manufacture started as family businesses, and some of the Tunbridge Ware workshops and showrooms can still be located round the town today. Jordan House, at the corner of Church Road, facing the Common, was one of these used by the Burrows family up to about 1845. Ireland mentions the name of Jordan, *an honest publican,* who, he claimed, had given Mount Ephraim and Mount Sion their names and *built the first house on this spot.*

Although the origin of Tunbridge Ware is not well documented, it is the town's oldest industry, carried on by a small number of families. It was first made as a sideline by woodworkers in nearby communities like Tonbridge and Speldhurst and sold to visitors to the Wells. By the 1770s, Tunbridge Ware was on sale, not only locally, but in London. The principal woods used at this time appear to have been holly, cherry, plum, yew and sycamore; and the manufacture of toys, small cabinets and souvenirs required skilled workmanship. The trade was still flourishing in the 19th century in the form of end-grain mosaic and marquetry, which largely superseded the earlier inlaid work. Patterns were made from thin sticks of wood assembled end-on into pre-designed blocks. They were then made into very thin veneers which were let into the surface of the article to be decorated, including boxes of all kinds, watchcases, chairs and tables. The designs varied from simple geometric patterns to floral compositions and highly finished landscapes. Princess Victoria was presented with a combined reading and writing stand and workbox in 1826, on her seventh birthday, by the inhabitants of the Wells in appreciation of her many visits. The industry declined at the turn of the century and finished in 1939. Today, the skilled craftsmanship of Tunbridge Ware is valued, and these articles are collectors' items.

In Ireland's brief account of the history of the Pantiles he does not mention the chapel (later a church) of King Charles the Martyr, possibly because of his antipathy to this *motley and frivolous monarch.* King Charles Church, opened for worship in 1678, was doubled in size in 1696. It is one of the oldest buildings in the town, and has changed little in 300 years. The simple galleried interior is furnished in dark oak, which contrasts with an elaborately plastered ceiling of shallow domes, richly decorated with wreaths of fruit, putti and leaf motifs. A fire in 1996 might well have destroyed this exquisite piece of workmanship by Sir Christopher Wren's chief plasterer, but the ceiling escaped with smoke damage only, and has been beautifully restored.

Neither is there any mention of Beau Nash in Ireland's account. This gentleman moved into the Wells from Bath in 1735, declared himself Master of Ceremonies and spent twenty-six energetic years regulating manners and imprinting his code of conduct on the Pantile Walks. Under his charismatic guidance, the Wells flourished. However, the advent of sea-bathing as a cure, and the proximity of Brighton, patronised by the youthful and exuberant Prince Regent, meant that the fortunes of the Wells, as a Spa town, declined. In 1779, Fanny Burney, staying at the Sussex Hotel en route for Brighton, described the Pantiles as having, 'no beauty in itself, only common houses at one side and little millinery and Tunbridge Ware shops at the other, and each end is choked up by buildings that intercept all prospect.'

However, the rising national prosperity of the 18th century meant that an increasing number of professional people and ex-service officers were looking for congenial surroundings in which to retire. These included Lord North, great-grandson of the man who discovered the waters, Lord Chief Justice Mansfield, and Lady Jerningham. Mansfield and Jerningham houses still stand on Mount Sion, taking the names of their original owners. These permanent residents helped the local economy, and the town grew and flourished, as did its reputation for respectability and cultured gentility. At the beginning of the 19th century, the four villages of the Walks (Pantiles), Mount Sion, Mount Ephraim-Culverden and Mount Pleasant-London Road, had not yet joined forces, but a building boom was soon under way. Shops and inns were refurbished near Mount Sion and the Walks, while a new garden city for the affluent rose up to the north, under the direction of the brilliant young architect, Decimus Burton (1800 - 1881). Between 1800 and 1841 the population had increased from 1,000 to over 8,000.

In 1845, the railway arrived, much to the delight of the citizens of Tunbridge Wells. The poor state of the roads had long been a bone of contention. Like many before him, Samuel Ireland was not impressed: *The depth of sand in the high roads renders them, at the season when the wells are most frequented, extremely unpleasant.* In spite of the Turnpike Acts of 1709 and 1711, the road from Tonbridge to the Wells remained unpleasant. Fanny Burney, in 1774, complained that the road was 'so very sidelum and jumblum', and touters on horse or foot intimidated visitors. The Central Station was completed in 1846 and a good rail service encouraged population growth which, by 1910, had risen to over 33,000.

The building boom continued in the 19th century with grandiose mansions such as those along the Pembury Road, Broadwater Down, Nevill and Hungershall Parks, as well as terraces and villas. Churches of every denomination soared heavenwards, the sign of a town that was both spiritually and economically healthy. One builder and developer, William Willicombe, was nicknamed the Cubitt of Tunbridge Wells, and the Gazette wrote, 'that he found Tunbridge Wells a town of moderate pretensions, and leaves it a fashionable watering place of palatial residences, second to few in the kingdom.' The crowning glory came in 1909 when King Edward VII permitted the town to become a Royal Spa.

The 20th century brought with it the blessing and the curse of the motorcar. In 1895, the enterprising mayor, Sir David Salomons, organised the first motor show of horseless carriages in England. One hundred years later, the town is choked with cars every day of the week, public transport is poor and there are no safe cycle lanes.

The declining and falling British Empire left a declining and falling residue of elderly, affluent ex-Empire builders. Many retired to the Royal Tunbridge Wells Spa, and spent their last years in the confines of the smarter hotels, and residential homes. The Pantiles, with the respectable but ageing department store, Dusts, at one end and the cafe, Binns, at the other, fossilized the image.

The famous Pantile Walks have been refurbished several times, most recently in the 1980s when the Corn Exchange and Lower Walk were virtually rebuilt. A permanent exhibition known as A Day at the Wells, is now housed in the Corn Exchange, advertised as recalling 'the sights, sounds and smells of Georgian Tunbridge Wells'. The name pantile, comes from the pans that were used to bake the bricks which paved the walks. Dusts has gone the way of all flesh, but Binns survives to fill hungry stomachs, if not with wheatears, at least with sticky buns. A draughty 1960s brick-and-glass edifice on stilts replaces the Pump House in Union Square. The Chalybeate Spring still exists where the Bath House once stood, and the dipper, a young lady in period costume, serves a mere four fluid ounces of rusty water to tourists.

In the high season, the Pantiles comes to life with a band, sedan-chair races, Shakespeare plays, Morris dancing and *Punch and Judy*. There is even a boules pitch

*The Chalybeate Spring, The Pantiles, Tunbridge Wells*

in the gravel, a game imported from France that would have disgusted Mr Ireland. Now, as in the 17th century, the Pantile Walks tend to be frequented mainly by tourists in the summer season.

The pedestrian shopping precinct in Calverley Road, with its new Victoria Place indoor shopping centre, attracts the young and the big spenders. Individual food shops have given way to supermarkets, and out-of-town superstores now overflow with shoppers who worship there on Sundays with the enthusiasm once reserved for the Church.

Although a large percentage of Tunbridge Wells citizens now commutes to London, it is not merely a dormitory town, for it provides schools, shops, hospitals and many other services for a large rural area. The 1991 census showed the population to be 45,145, and the town continues to grow both in size and prosperity. Mr Ireland might well have recognised the view from Mount Ephraim, where 18th century houses still stare condescendingly across the town and common to the rolling countryside beyond. Lying among seven hills, and built round its original common, it remains, in essence, the same place that Benge-Burr described 200 years ago: 'at a little distance, it bears the appearance of a town in the midst of woods and conveys to the imagination the soothing idea of a rural romantic settlement, while it actually affords all the conveniences of a city life.'

# Bayham Abbey

*From Tunbridge Wells our river Medway, in a very narrow stream, winds its spiral course towards the elegant remains of Bayham Abbey . . . The cluttered Gothic pillars, the broken pointed arches and richly sculptured ornaments, all mouldering into decay and tufted here and there with the shaggy moss and creeping ivy, render it an assemblage of objects equally beautiful in the eye of the painter, and the contemplation of the moralist. Lo!*

'Passion sleeps while mouldering ruins speak;
Methinks I hear some furrowed monk relate,
What frenzy urg'd to Bayham's still retreat;
With vain regret, in pensive mood declare
I fought at Agincourt, my trade was war;
But quitting honor, and ambition's road,
Sought an asylum in this house of God.'

Ireland's *very narrow stream* is not the Medway at all, but the River Teise. This tributary rises in Waterdown Forest, south of Tunbridge Wells and joins the Medway at Twyford Bridge, Yalding.

So Ireland finishes his *Picturesque Views,* as he started them, at an abbey. Bayham, unlike Minster Abbey on the Isle of Sheppey, is sited in a fertile, undulating landscape. The River Teise chuckles beneath the overhanging branches of alder and willow, looping round hop-gardens and bluebell woods. The *elegant remains* of Bayham Abbey, with its great lake, rise from rich, green pastures, surrounded by wooded hills and welcome tranquillity.

The Abbey was well-sited by the Premonstratensian Canons who settled here in 1290. This Order was founded by St Norbert in 1121 at Premonstre, near Laon in northern France. The monks were known as White Canons, for they wore a white cloak and cassock. The story goes that the Virgin Mary appeared in a dream to the founder of the Order and indicated the spot where She wished Her Abbey to be built in France. This is borne out by the name, 'prae' meaning before, and 'monstre' to show.

Only twenty-two years after the foundation of the Order, the White Canons came to England to establish the first Premonstratensian Abbey at Newhouse, Lincolnshire. Soon the Order had over thirty abbeys and priories in England. In the 14th century these Norburtian or White Canons were sent out to work in the diocesan parishes without losing contact with their abbey or priory. Perhaps all this interaction with the sinful world made the Bayham brotherhood lax in the observance of monastic rules, for they grew fat with good living. Thomas Cottingham, who was abbot during the mid-15th century, was deposed after a visitation by the Bishop of Chichester who found the brothers living far too well, and complained of them wearing pointed shoes 'such as befitted a fop rather than a brother'. He revisited in 1491 and found things little better, one of the Order 'staying out of nights' while another was an apostate. During an excavation of the ruins in the 1970s, a cache of pointed shoes was discovered near the monastic latrines, no doubt hastily hidden from the prying eyes of inspecting bishops.

In 1525, Bayham Abbey was suppressed, along with a number of supposedly unworkable monasteries. Ireland writes . . . *this abbey . . . became one of the first that Cardinal Wolsey laid his clutches on, to enable him to prosecute the plan of founding his Colleges of Ipswich and Oxford.*

No provision was made for the redundant and spirited canons of Bayham, so they joined forces in a riot with the discharged servants and some of the local populace reoccupying the buildings, and electing one, Thomas Towers, as abbot. The ringleaders of this 'unseemly riot', (or miniature 'Pilgrimage of Grace', depending whose side you were on), were imprisoned, and the abbey remained empty and unmolested until 1714. It was then purchased by Sir John Pratt, Chief Justice of the King's Bench, who probably thought of it as an investment for his retirement rather than for a residence. His steward, anticipating his master's wishes, unroofed the complete transept which had been used, possibly as a barn. Pratt died in 1725, and his grandson, the 2nd Lord Camden, inherited the abbey in 1797.

Samuel Ireland, obsequious as ever, continues in his flowery prose:

*Amidst these charming ruins, Mr. Pratt, their owner, has built a good house, and somewhat in the Gothic style, that it may assimilate with the taste of the adjoining ruins. This gentleman is nephew to Earl Camden, a name distinguished in the annals of this country, and deeply impressed in the breast of every Englishman who admires the fabric of our excellent constitution.*

He was probably referring to the Ist Earl Camden, who became Lord Chancellor in 1766, never owning the property, although he took the title of Viscount Bayham. It was John Pratt of Bayham, who built the villa which forms the northern part of the present Dower House, and was a pioneer of pre-Romantic Gothic taste. In 1752 Horace Walpole admired the building, which supposedly gave him inspiration for his Gothic mansion at Strawberry Hill. In the 1990s, the Gothic north end of the Dower House is used for weddings, christenings, and meetings. Watched over by the ancient ruins, couples take their vows in the upper room before adjourning to a marquee for the wedding breakfast. When the sun sets, the floodlit ruins reverberate to the sound of secular music.

In the latter part of the 18th and 19th centuries, the ruins, with a little help from the fashionable landscape gardener, Humphrey Repton, were moulded into a 'picturesque' Gothic- revival landscape. Lakes, reflecting the ruins, were dug on the east side, ivy-leaved toadflax was encouraged to grow over the sandstone walls of the abbey itself, and a number of picturesque drawings, like Ireland's, record the ruins in the 1770s and 1780s.

In 1870, the mansion known as Bayham House was built for the Marquess Camden by the architect, David Brandon, in the Gothic style of the times. Cresting the hill on the far side of the valley to the west, it dominates the abbey.

Today, the old gatehouse marks the boundary of Kent, covering the road from the north and the abbey estate of Little Sandhurst. Although the reed-filled boating lake has now dried up, the gatehouse makes a romantic ruin beside the fish-filled waters of the Teise, crossed by an arched, stone bridge.

*The old gatehouse, Bayham Abbey*

The considerable remains of the abbey are still dramatic. Cleared of ivy, the golden sandstone ruins soar joyfully upwards, the high vaulting, moulded arches and graceful pillars give an enduring sense of exuberance and certainty in God the Creator. The long narrow nave, with three of the six bays still standing to parapet height, is awesome. A green corridor leads to the high altar where the leaves of a mature beech tree trace a natural east window. The gnarled roots of this great tree pour over the stone wall behind the altar, a perfect setting for late 20th century weddings, and a tribute to Humphrey Repton's romantic ideals.

The green and gold valley, set amidst wooded hills, perfectly complements the luminous sandstone of the ancient abbey. The rays of the setting sun set the stones on fire, Man in Nature at the still point of a turning world.

Samuel Ireland concludes his book with a tribute to the "Men of Kent":

*I cannot, however, take leave of the banks of this River, fertile and beautiful as I have found it in every part, without paying an equal tribute of respect and admiration to that high character by which the Men of Kent have been so renowned above those of every other part of our much-envied island. Time has done away the suspicion of flattery on their part, and truth, by the consent of ages, has stamped an indelible authority on their names.*

The book ends with the following verse by an unnamed *elegant writer of the present century*, which encapsulates the historic discord between France and England at the end of the 18th century:

Now on fair Dover's topmost cliff I'll stand,

And look with scorn and triumph on proud France.

Of yore an isthmus, jutting from this coast,

Join'd the Brittannic to the Gallic shore;

But Neptune on a day, with fury fir'd,

Rear'd his tremendous trident, smote the earth,

And broke the unnatural union at a blow. -

"Twixt you and you, my servants and my sons,

Be there (he cried) eternal discord. - France

Shall bow the neck to Cantium's peerless offspring,

And as the oak reigns lordly o'er the shrub,

So shall the hop have homage from the vine."

As the millennium approaches, the European Union attempts to bind the historic wounds between France and Britain. Concord, rather than discord is the watchword. Monetary union is about to become a reality, and shoals of Britons quench their thirst on wine and beer imported from France. Standing on Dover's *topmost cliff* today, Mr Ireland would see the glittering ventilation shafts of the Channel Tunnel and wonder at the large number of French tourists who pour into Kent to visit many of the *venerable* buildings he describes in his *Picturesque Views on the Medway*.

# Bibliography

Barnard, Dereck, *Merrily to Frendsbury.* A City of Rochester Society publication.

Benge-Burr, Thomas, *A Guide to Tunbridge Wells,* 1766.

Biggs, Howard, *The River Medway,* Published by Terence Dalton Ltd. 1982.

Bignell, Alan, *Hopping Down in Kent.* Robert Hale Ltd. 1977.

Booklets: Leeds, Hever, Penshurst, Groombridge, Cooling (Rochester Visitor's Centre leaflet), Temple Manor Strood, Upnor Castle (English Heritage), Bayham Abbey (English Heritage). Malling Abbey 1997, Rochester Castle (English Heritage).

Church, Richard, *Kent,* Robert Hale Ltd.

Coles-Finch, William, *In Kentish Pilgrim Land* The C.W. Daniel Company. 1925.

Coombe, Derek, *The Bawleymen.*

*Country Life*, 23 October 1958, Nettlestead Place, Kent I & II.

Dickens, Charles, *Great Expectations, Edwin Drood.*

Goodsall, Robert H., *The Medway.* Constable, London. 1955.

Guildhall Museum, Rochester.

Hall, Elizabeth, *The Garden of England, Kent. Evolution of Historic Gardens in Kent.*

*Haysden Country Park Historical Trail*, Tonbridge and Malling Borough Council.

Hasted, Edward, *History and Topographical Survey in the County of Kent*, 1782.

Hetherington, Keith, Griffiths, Alun, *Old Pubs of Tunbridge Wells & District.*

*History of the Ashes,* Cobham Hall 1998 & Guided Historic Tour Handbook, 1994.

Hughes, David T., *Sheerness and the Mutuny at the Nore.*

Humble Richard, *The Saxon Kings,* Book Club Associates, London.

Hunt, Ann, *Engravings of Kent.* Robert Hale. 1989.

Igglesden, Sir Charles, *A Saunter Through Kent,* published 1934.

Ireland, Samuel, *Picturesque Views on the River Medway.* T. & J. Edgerton, Whitehall 1793.

Jessup, F.W, *A History of Kent.* Phillimore & Co. Ltd. 1995.

Lawrence, Margaret, *A Bridge Over the Stream,* East Peckham Parish Council. 1995.

MacDougall, Philip, *Chatham Dockyard in Old Photographs.* Alan Sutton Pub. Ltd.

MacDougall, Philip, *The Hoo Peninsula.* Alan Sutton Publishing Ltd.

Mair, John, *The Fourth Forger,* Cobden-Sanderson. 1938.

Maxwell, Donald, *Unknown Kent,* John Lane, The Bodley Head Ltd. 1921.

Maycock, Alan, *St. Mary's Abbey, West Malling.* 1953.

*Medway Bridges, Eight Historic Prints*, K.C.C. 1978.

Medway Heritage Centre, Chatham.

*Medway Queen, The Survivor*. Published by Medway Queen Preservation Society

Medway Study Centre, Strood.

*Medway Valley Walk*, K.C.C., 1996.

Mee, Arthur, *The King's England, Kent*. Hodder & Stoughton. New Edition 1969.

Meresborough Books.

*National Dictionary of Biography*.

*N.R.A., River Medway Catchment Management Plan Final Report* - July 1993

Ogly, Bob, *In the Wake of the Hurricane*, 1987.

Orchard, Barry, *A Look at the Head and the Fifty*, James & James Publishers Ltd. 1991.

Pears Cyclopaedia.

Pepys Samuel, Diary.

Preston, J. M., *Industrial Medway - an historical survey*. 1977.

Penn, Roger, *Portrait of the River Medway*, Robert Hale. London. 1981.

Pritchett, Bill, *Cobham*, Revised 1991.

Prosser, Arthur, *Illustrated History of Kent*.

Rowse, A.L., *The Story of Britain*. Tiger Books International 1979.

Russell, J.M., *The History of Maidstone*, John Hallewell Publications. Rep 1978 of 1881 ed.

*Saint Norburt, Great Moments in the History of Christianity*. Univers Media.

Savidge, Alan, *Royal Tunbridge Wells*. Midas Books. 1975.

Smith, F.F., *A History of Rochester*. John Hallewell Publications, 1976.

Sprange, J., *The Tunbridge Wells Guide*, 1786

Stead, Richard, *Bygone Kent*. First pub. 1892. Republished by E.P. Publishing Ltd 1972.

Sunday Telegraph 3.5.1998

Waldron, Smithers David, *Castles in Kent*, John Hallewell Publications 1980.

Watson, Hilary, *The Book of Maidstone*. Barracuda 1981.

World Book Encyclopaedia.